Fruit of the Spirit - Bible Stuay

cultivating and understanding the fruit of the spirit and how it can and should be manifested in our lives

FruitoftheSpiritSeries.com
By: Lara Velez, Founder of Moms of Faith

Table of Contents

Introduction

But the fruit of the Spirit is love, joy, peace, longsuffering, gentleness, goodness, faith, meekness, temperance: against such there is no law. And they that are Christ's have crucified the flesh with the affections and lusts. If we live in the Spirit, let us also walk in the Spirit. - Galatians 5:22-23

Unfortunately, many in the church today have no clue what the Fruit of the Spirit is or how significant it is. It is not only important to learn about it and walk in the spirit, it is equally important to search for it in others. The Word clearly tells us that we will know them (other Believers) by their fruit.

When we give our lives to Christ and allow Him to be Lord of our lives. We begin our Christian walk. As we grow in the Lord we also grow "fruit" (or spiritual qualities). The closer we get in our relationship with God the more we recognize sin in our lives, and the more uncomfortable we become with it. If we are growing we will bear good fruit and the manifestation will be the character qualities found in Galatians 5. We will also become more aware of our fleshly tendencies and desire to turn from them.

On the flip side, if we decide to "go our own way," and not allow God to work in our lives, we will gradually become desensitized and not even recognize what is sin and what is not. That is what is happening to the Church today. The Church is becoming "liberal." Meaning, it is picking and choosing what is and should be called "sin" for our "times." We have forgotten the God and His Word are the same yesterday, today, and FOREVER! God does not "change" for man or "times."

If you want to bear good fruit, submit and obey God and HIS Word, NOT the world's interpretation of what it "should" be to fit its sinful nature and desires.

You can also know if someone is truly God's by what comes out of them. Does it line up with the Word? Do they bear good fruit? Or, do they try to adapt the Word with the "times" we live in? Be VERY careful of those wolves. They are everywhere, even in the Church…

Beware of false prophets, who come to you dressed as sheep, but inside they are devouring wolves. You will fully recognize them by their fruits. Do people pick grapes from thorns, or figs from thistles? Even so, every healthy (sound) tree bears good fruit, but the sickly (decaying, worthless) tree bears bad (worthless) fruit. A good (healthy) tree cannot bear bad (worthless) fruit, nor can a bad (diseased) tree bear excellent fruit. Every tree that does not bear good fruit is cut down and cast into the fire. Therefore, you will fully know them by their fruits. Not everyone who says to Me, Lord, Lord, will enter the kingdom of heaven, but he who does the will of My Father Who is in heaven. Many will say to Me on that day, Lord, Lord, have we not prophesied in Your name and driven out demons in Your name and done many mighty works in Your name? And then I will say to them openly (publicly), I never knew you; depart from Me, you who act wickedly [disregarding My commands]. - Matthew 7:15-23

Sadly, I have encountered many "Christians" who are really wolves and bear no good fruit. Sure, they play a good game and have the appearance or illusion of godliness. However, they are really suffering from a rotten core and their trees only appear to be full of beautiful fruit. The sad reality is that on the inside they are decaying, ugly, and devour everything good in their path.

Be diligent and aware of these people and the condition of your own heart as well… lest you become one of these with rotten cores.

We battle not with flesh and blood, but with powers and principalities. We have a very real battle with our flesh and spirit. In this Bible study, we will dig deeper into the Fruit of the Spirit and how to walk fully in the spirit.

For we are not fighting against flesh-and-blood enemies, but against evil rulers and authorities of the unseen world, against mighty powers in this dark world, and against evil spirits in the heavenly places. Therefore, put on every piece of God's armor so you will be able to resist the enemy in the time of evil. Then after the battle you will still be standing firm. - Ephesians 6:12-13

Part of our armor and ability to battle our flesh is to learn how to <u>walk in the spirit</u>.

Let's pray:

Lord, thank You for Your Word. Help me to remember all that I learn in this study, and remind me when I need a refresher course. I love You so very much. I want my life to be a living example of Your Grace, Love, and Mercy. I want others to see Your Light shining brightly through me. I want to walk in the spirit and cut out my fleshly and sinful nature. Teach me, Lord. I am the clay and YOU are the Potter. Mold me into the beautiful, fruit bearing tree, that You created me to be. Thank You for Your Word and Your unfailing Love. In Jesus' Mighty Name, Amen.

Fruit of Self-Control

But the fruit of the Spirit is love, joy, peace, longsuffering, gentleness, goodness, faith, Meekness, **temperance:** *against such there is no law. And they that are Christ's have crucified the flesh with the affections and lusts. If we live in the Spirit, let us also walk in the Spirit.* - Galatians 5:22-23

This will be a fun one... In the original Greek **temperance** is **egkrateia** *(eng-krat'-i-ah)* and means **SELF CONTROL**.

I struggle with anger in my life. It is my "Achilles heel" as it were. Through much prayer and study I have come to the realization that I may struggle with it my whole life. However, I also know that I have been given the power to <u>overcome</u> sin (lack of self control) through the shed Blood of Jesus Christ. I have been given the power of the Holy Spirit to help me live a holy life and <u>manifest the Fruit of the Spirit</u>.

Self Control is the key to me overcoming my battle with anger. It is the key to many of our human struggles; overeating, cigarettes, alcohol, poor choices, emotional outburst and all of our "bad habits".

We have a choice in everything. God did not create us to be puppets on a string. He gave us <u>freedom of choice</u>; not only to accept Jesus as our Savior but in how we conduct ourselves in life. "The devil made me do it" is a bunch of bologna. The devil cannot "make" us do anything. The only thing that he can do is tempt us. It is then <u>our choice</u> to resist temptation or give in. It is definitely our choice all the way.

When <u>we choose</u> to lose control we have made the conscious choice to sin. It does not have to be that way. Once we become saved we have power over sin in our lives. **We no longer have to give in to the desires of the flesh.** That is why *self control* is a Fruit of the Spirit. It is a character trait that we **develop** *as we exercise our position in*

Christ and obey God. I strongly recommend that you read Romans 6. Paul went into great detail regarding our freedom from sin.

Choosing Self Control

Self control is a choice. We may fail at times. Ultimately, though, it is still a **choice we must make**. It is not something that will come easily. Sure, there may be certain aspects of our lives that are easier to keep under control than others; however, I am pretty certain each of us have at least one area we struggle to control in our life.

> When our spouse annoys us, we can **choose** to let it go and remember how much we love them.

> When our children drive us nuts, we can **choose** to show them love and mercy instead of screaming and yelling.

> When life gets rough, we can **choose** to trust in the One Who loves us more than His own life and believe what His Word says.

> When temptation comes knocking, we can **choose** to avoid it and even run from it instead of giving in and saying, *"I just can't..."*

Yes, we can! If we are saved, we have the power of the Living God living IN us!

Technically, we have the freedom to do anything we want to do in life. However, when we choose to walk in sin, we are walking away from all the good that God has planned for our lives. It is all about **our choices** and perseverance. God's Word says that He will keep no good thing from us...

For the Lord God is our sun and our shield. He gives us grace and glory. The Lord will withhold no good thing from those who do what is right. - Psalm 84:11

...and He doesn't. We do. We make the wrong choices. We say the wrong things. We make the choice. *We do or don't do...*

Everything has two sides. Everything in life is a choice.

You can be born in poverty and still become the president of a multi million dollar company…

You can start out in life uneducated and still overcome and find success…

You can grow up like me: in financial destitution, with an alcoholic father and endure <u>years</u> of sexual abuse from dirty men; still follow God's path, and become a successful author and the founder of one of the most popular websites for Christian Moms…

*…You can overcome any obstacle in life--**if** you choose to make the right choices.*

We can do ALL things (<u>including manifest self-control in our lives</u>) through Christ Who gives us strength! The Word says ALL, not some…ALL. *(ref. Philippians 4:13)*

No matter where you are in life or what your struggles are, *you can make a decision right now to make your life better simply by making better choices every day*. **Self control** is gaining control of your anger, hurts, past mistakes, bitterness, poverty, self pity, unhappiness, etc., and choosing to lay it all at the foot of the Cross. Then, picking yourself up (sometimes daily), <u>moving forward and choosing to take your life and attitudes in a new direction</u>: the direction that God has already planned out and paved for you while you were still in your mother's womb!

All you have to do is choose to walk it.

The Choice...

The choosing part is what becomes tricky. How do we choose not to deck someone in the heat of the moment? How do we choose to shut our mouth when someone hurts our feelings? How do we choose to walk away from a strong temptation?

How?

Well, there are several factors that must be in place...

> **We must have an active prayer life.** This means being in daily contact with the Lord. Sharing our struggles, repenting of sin, thanking Him for all He does. This is all vital to building a relationship with Him.

> **Read the Word Daily.** If we are not in the Word, we will have no clue Who we serve. Know Him by reading and meditating on His Love Letter to YOU.

> **Choosing to stay away from** people, places and things that cause you to stray or encourage you to veer off course.

> **Accountability.** It is important to have someone in your life who is more spiritually mature than you are, so that you can get good advice, prayer, encouragement, or even a much needed reality check.

> **Get up off the floor when you fall on your face**! Understand that there is a 99.9999% chance that you will fail...if not 100%. The only way to overcome is to never *ever* give up!

You see, it is all in our hands. *We need to make a decision to walk in the Spirit and allow the Lord to work in us and **prune** what He wants to prune in our lives.* Then and only then can we come to a place where we can actually SEE the fruit of Self-Control working in our lives.

Gain Control of our Thought Life

I am convinced that we overlook our thought life to the degree that many of our strongholds are rooted there. Every sin we commit *begins as a thought*. We must first think it, before we do it.

> **Example 1:** Our friend gets a new gadget that we have been pining for over the course of several months. When they are sharing their excitement, instead of feeling happy for them, we begin to get annoyed and *wonder* why "they" get everything and we don't. Before you know it, we are irritated with this poor person who has done nothing wrong, and we are coveting THEIR blessing. So, not only are we jealous, envious and bitter, we are allowing a root to *form in our minds*. This root may later manifest itself as a hurtful comment, gossip or even downright alienation of this person. Why? We allowed our minds to be controlled by sin instead of taking control of our minds. Control that was given to us through the shed Blood of Jesus Christ!

> **Example 2:** Our spouse lies to us about something. They did not come clean—they were caught red handed in the lie. We start *thinking* about everything else they do wrong and wonder what else they are keeping from us. They apologize and ask us to forgive them. We decide we would rather seethe and hold on to the offense for awhile. Unfortunately, we are not hurting anyone but ourselves with this method. We should forgive as we are forgiven. We should show the grace and mercy we so readily beg for when we mess up…A root of bitterness will take hold of us and soon we will find ourselves in the midst of a very troubled marriage. Why? Because WE decided that we knew better than God and chose not to pardon another's sin— as our sins are so freely pardoned when we repent to our Lord and Savior…

I can offer many examples from our jobs, to more marriage scenarios, to what we watch, to how we feel about ourselves and others and so on. However, the above examples give you something to think about and see how it all begins: in the **mind**.

It is vital that we gain control of what we allow in, and what we allow our minds to think on.

And now, dear brothers and sisters, one final thing. Fix your thoughts on what is true, and honorable, and right, and pure, and lovely, and admirable. Think about things that are excellent and worthy of praise. - Philippians 4:8

This Scripture has become my life Scripture. I am constantly referring to it. It really helps me overcome a LOT. It was not put in the Word by accident. God knows us and understands how the mind works. He also gave us the power to overcome sin and put our minds under the submission of Christ.

Be well balanced (temperate, sober of mind), be vigilant and cautious at all times; for that enemy of yours, the devil, roams around like a lion roaring in fierce hunger, seeking someone to seize upon and devour. - 1 Peter 5:8

Our enemy knows our weaknesses, and will take every opportunity to exploit them and set us up for failure. He is not playing around. He seriously wants us to fall flat on our face! That is why it is **vital** that we are on *constant watch*.

For the weapons of our warfare are not carnal but mighty in God for pulling down strongholds, casting down arguments and every high thing that exalts itself against the knowledge of God, bringing every thought into captivity to the obedience of Christ. - 2 Corinthians 10:4-5

As I read these verses, it became clear that it is OUR job to take control of our own minds.

How can we do this?

The answer is both simple and complicated. It requires **effort** on our parts. We must be on constant guard. We must pay attention to what we are thinking about and lay down all that is impure, unlovely, and wrong at the Feet of Jesus. We must be careful what we allow in as well. For example; if all we are watching, reading and listening to is sinful garbage, what do we expect to come from it?

Sadly, garbage will only beget garbage…

I cannot say this enough: we **must** pay attention to what we are thinking about. We **must** spend time in the Word—daily. Then, we will have something powerful to replace any sinful thoughts that come our way. Ask God to reveal to you anything in your life that could be contributing to any mind battles.

Every time…EVERY time a sinful thought sneaks in, we need to rebuke it and replace it with *"what is true, and honorable, and right, and pure, and lovely, and admirable. Think about things that are excellent and worthy of praise."*

The Wages of Sin...

Let no one say when he is tempted, I am tempted from God; for God is incapable of being tempted by evil and He Himself tempts no one.

*But every person is tempted when he is drawn away, enticed and baited **by his own evil desires**.*

Then the evil desire, when it has conceived, gives birth to sin, and sin, when fully matured, brings forth death. - James 1:13-15

Many times, when we are tempted, we have this need to put the blame anywhere *except the image in the mirror*. We not only put the blame on God, but we put it on the world, our spouses, our children, other people, the way we were raised, our past hurts, society, circumstances we endured--and of course, the most common one: the devil.

The truth is that God has given us freedom of choice, and if we choose to be tempted astray--then we will be. We are the ones that get drawn away. We are the ones with the evil thoughts and desires. We allow ourselves to be baited.

When we allow it to go from a thought to an action--we sin, and when we sin, we are opening the door to death and destruction. This doesn't necessarily mean we physically die. Depending on the sin, it could mean the death of a relationship, finances, dreams, job, and of course physical death.

The only way to really overcome temptation is to renew our mind. The only way we can renew our mind is to study the Word. **Every sin that we commit starts in our mind.** When we allow our minds to go astray, we are opening the door to sin and death. This does not have to happen. God has given us **power over sin**. God has shown us through His Word how to *overcome sin* and death.

However, it is our choice. We can choose to be overcome by temptations, or we can choose to overcome temptation. We must submit our thought life to Him and stop the thought before it ever becomes a manifestation.

*For the **wages of sin is death**, but the free gift of God is eternal life through Christ Jesus our Lord.* — Romans 6:23

Obedience

*Submit yourselves therefore to God. **Resist** the devil, and he **will** flee from you. - James 4:7*

God always gives us the resources we need to live victorious lives. Many times, for various reasons, we just don't use them. James is telling us yet another way to <u>overcome</u> the enemy.

If we **choose** to live obedient lives, we gain power--the power to drive the enemy away simply by resisting him. He will literally vanish from us. That doesn't mean he will never return. We will have to resist him until we die or Jesus comes back (whichever comes first).

Obedience to God helps us to more readily want to resist the devil. When we are walking in the flesh, we rarely even recognize temptations. Why? Because we are giving into them so much that we become desensitized. On the flip side, if we are walking in the spirit and living lives submitted to the Father, then we know and recognize when the enemy comes knocking…

…and when we resist him, he leaves us because he knows that we will no longer entertain his foolishness in that area of our lives. The tricky part is to be submitted with our whole life--not just pieces of it. You see, we can be submitted in one area and have no problem resisting the devil. Then, be completely out of alignment in another area: constantly battling him unsuccessfully.

If we choose to live obedient lives, it will be something we must pursue day by day and minute by minute. It is a <u>constant decision</u> to do God's Will and not our own. When we really get that and put it into practice, we will have many more victories than defeats.

Living for Eternity

"Do not think that I have come to abolish the Law or the Prophets; I have not come to abolish them but to fulfill them.

I tell you the truth, until heaven and earth disappear, not the smallest letter, not the least stroke of a pen, will by any means disappear from the Law until everything is accomplished.

Anyone who breaks one of the least of these commandments and teaches others to do the same will be called least in the kingdom of heaven, but whoever practices and teaches these commands will be called great in the kingdom of heaven.

For I tell you that unless your righteousness surpasses that of the Pharisees and the teachers of the law, you will certainly not enter the kingdom of heaven. - Matthew 5:17-20

I have always been fascinated by the fact that there will be "positions" in Heaven. And we choose what they will be by our actions here on earth. If we waste our time here on our fleshly, sinful desires and make excuses to continue in our sin, we will spend eternity regretting it.

Don't get me wrong, we will be in Heaven, and Heaven will be a MUCH better place than hell.

However...

My question is: do you want to be one of the least? For ETERNITY?! It's not like we can come back and change it all. We make our choices every day, while we are here on earth. Every time we choose to walk in the spirit and live obedient lives, we are not only storing up our eternal treasure, but we are choosing the position that we will hold for ETERNITY! On the flip side: every time we sow the seed of fleshly living, we are demoting our potential position in Heaven.

I refuse to be a chamber maid in Heaven! I want to *have all* and *be all* that God created me to be! I want to walk through those Pearly Gates and hear my Daddy say, *"WELL DONE!"* I want my eternity to be the very BEST that it can be.

Don't you want all that God has for you? Not only here on earth, but for eternity? You can have it all, my friends. You really can. All you have to do is live your life for the One Who sticks closer than a brother. The One Who will NEVER leave you or forsake you. The One Who loves you more than His Own life and comfort.

It really is a no-brainer!

Live right!

DIE to the flesh!

Let go of sin and grab hold of the KING OF KINGS!

Back to the Basics

Let's go back to the beginning…

Self-Control

It means; *restraint exercised over one's own impulses, emotions, or desires. It is self-discipline, self-restraint, willpower, level headedness.*

Think about what we would be like if we lacked self control…

We would be out of control.

Think about a car. When it hits speeds over 80mph, it does not take much to lose control of it. One wrong move from the driver… one slippery puddle… and that car can spin out of control and cause chaos and destruction to everything in its path.

We need to make sure that we are not only remaining within the boundaries that our loving Father created for us (do the speed limit), we need to remain in control of our vehicle (hearts, minds, choices…lives).

We choose.

Self-Control is not easy to come by. However, it CAN be a regular part of our lives—IF we are willing to remain close in our relationship with our Lord and Savior, and allow our flesh to hurt a little…sometimes a lot.

You see, when we are walking WITH Him regularly, it is very hard to remain in sin. We get convicted and we feel ashamed. The key is to recognize the trigger points, and either eliminate them or be diligent in keeping them at bay.

Self-Control.

Out of Control.

What will you choose?

Self Control - Study Guide

Let's Pray:

Lord, thank You for Your life giving Word. Thank You that Your Word holds all the answers. Help me to separate my ideas and thoughts from the world's. Help me to adapt and submit my life, thoughts, and feelings to what Your Word says. Help me to develop the fruit of self control by living an obedient, submitted, and consecrated life. Thank You for Your Son and the living example that He lived. Thank You...Thank You... Praise You! In Jesus' Mighty Name, Amen!

Memorize:

If you really love Me, you will obey My commands. – John 14:15

Dig Deeper:

An obedient and submitted life will reap blessings. On the contrary, a disobedient and SELF lived life will reap destruction.

Do not be deceived, deluded, and misled; God will not allow Himself to be sneered at or mocked by mere pretensions or professions, or by His precepts being set aside. He inevitably deludes himself who attempts to delude God. For whatever a man sows, that and that only is what he will reap - Galatians 6:7

Let us not be deceived into thinking that God's Word can be adapted to the current culture, or that we only have to pick and choose the areas we agree with to obey. Jesus said in John 14:15 *"If you really love Me, you will obey My commands."*

We serve such an Awesome, Loving and Mighty God. He does so much for us every day. He sent His Son so we can live with Him in Eternity. As if all He did and does was not enough, He left us an Instruction Manual for life!

Every Scripture is God-breathed (given by His inspiration) and profitable for instruction, for reproof and conviction of sin, for correction of error and discipline in obedience, and for training in righteousness (in holy living, in conformity to God's will in thought, purpose, and action), So that the man of God may be complete and proficient, well fitted and thoroughly equipped for every good work. - 2 Timothy 3:16-17

The Word of God is far more than a mere book. It is a manual for life. It is filled with instructions from cover to cover on how to live, love, overcome and become obedient children who lack no good thing. It teaches us God's ways and how to find strength to make better choices. It also shows us the way to mercy and forgiveness. It equips us for life in this sinful world. It is something every Christian should study and know well.

So brace up your minds; be sober (morally alert); set your hope wholly and unchangeably on the grace that is coming to you when Jesus Christ is revealed. Live as children of obedience to God; do not conform yourselves to the evil desires that governed you in your former ignorance, when you did not know the requirements of the Gospel. But as the One Who called you is holy, you yourselves also be holy in all your conduct and manner of living. - 1 Peter 1:13-15

How do we live holy lives that are obedient to God?

Receive Christ as our Savior.

Study God's Word to KNOW HIS ways.

Be Teachable. Allow the Holy Spirit to teach you by listening for His still small voice.

Pray Often.

Trust His Word.

Submit to God's Will.

Let go of sin and unhealthy things.

Understand that anything God asks us to give up is for our own good.

Forgive others.

Forgive yourself.

Walk in the spirit by knowing His Word and living it.

Resist the devil.

Love others.

Spend TIME with God.

Praise His Holy Name.

Study, study, study!

Studying is a major key to obedient living. If we do not KNOW God's Word, how can we obey His precepts??

Study and be eager and do your utmost to present yourself to God approved, a workman who has no cause to be ashamed, correctly analyzing and accurately dividing [rightly handling and skillfully teaching] the Word of Truth. - 2 Timothy 2:15

Do not misunderstand; God loves you "as is." However, we must grow. If we do not grow, we are unhealthy. Obeying Him is LOVING HIM FOR WHO HE IS. Obeying Him is the path to peace, right living, health, effectiveness and happiness.

Of whom we have much to say, and hard to explain, since you have become dull of hearing. For though by this time you ought to be teachers, you need someone to teach you again the first principles of the oracles of God; and you have come to need milk and not solid food. For everyone who partakes only of milk is unskilled in the word of righteousness, for he is a babe. But solid food belongs to those who are of full age, that is, those who by reason of use have their senses exercised to discern both good and evil. - Hebrews 5:11-14

We need to grow up.

It would be sad to see one of our grown children walking around in diapers... It would be even worse if WE are still in diapers! Let's study God's Word, start obeying it and allowing Him to TEACH us through it, so we can GROW up into the men and women He created us to be!

Scripture Study:

Look up the following Scriptures. I encourage you to really dig deep here and study them, look up any references and pray over them!

- 2 Peter 1:5-7
- Proverbs 25:28
- Titus 2:11-14

- 1 Corinthians 10:13
- Romans 12:2
- 1 Corinthians 9:24-27
- 2 Timothy 1:7
- Titus 1:8
- Matthew 6:33
- Deuteronomy 8:20
- Galatians 5:16-26
- Matthew 6:24
- Psalm 119:112
- Psalm 119:60
- Acts 5:29
- 1 Peter 1:14
- Ephesians 5:11
- Philippians 2:12
- Psalm 112:1
- Proverbs 16:7
- 1 John 2:17
- James 2:24
- Luke 11:28
- Mark 3:35
- Matthew 25:20-23
- Matthew 26:41

Also, for an even deeper study, look up the following words in your concordance, and study the Scripture references: *obedience, submitted, and consecrated.*

Fruit of Meekness

But the fruit of the Spirit is love, joy, peace, longsuffering, gentleness, goodness, faith, meekness, temperance: against such there is no law. And they that are Christ's have crucified the flesh with the affections and lusts. If we live in the Spirit, let us also walk in the Spirit. - **Galatians 5:22-23**

The original Greek word for **meekness** is **praos** (prah'-os) and means gentle, humble, gentleness

This is a very important character trait to develop in life. We must learn how to manifest gentleness towards our spouses, friends, strangers, family, and so on. **We must conduct ourselves with a gentle and merciful attitude and speech.** Harshness is something we should avoid. It will gain us nothing and only hurt those around us.

We need to remember that we reap what we sow. For instance; if we sow harshness we will reap harshness. If we sow kindness, mercy, and gentleness… we will receive kindness, mercy, and gentleness.

Do not be deceived and deluded and misled; God will not allow Himself to be sneered at (scorned, disdained, or mocked by mere pretensions or professions, or by His precepts being set aside.) He inevitably deludes himself who attempts to delude God. For whatever a man sows, that and that only is what he will reap. - *Galatians 6:7*

We must also remember that the fruit of the spirit are not easily obtained. Walking in the spirit requires a willingness to submit our lives to the Authority of Christ, walk in discipline, and die to our flesh daily—even minute by minute if necessary!

Pride Hinders Meekness

Pride can be very dangerous and can also destroy our ability to walk in meekness.

Have you ever heard a sermon or teaching and immediately felt annoyed, or maybe like this was definitely NOT a message for you?

I have.

Now, there have been times, when the message was just downright nutty. However, that is rare. Most of the time (especially since I am VERY careful about whom I allow to speak into my life), it is right on the money.

*Pride goes before destruction and a haughty spirit before a fall. Better it is to be of a **humble** spirit with the **meek** and poor than to divide the spoil with the proud. – Proverbs 16:18-19*

Pride is destructive to the person who holds the pride. Pride prevents us from hearing God's Truth and learning what He wants us to learn. Pride is a terrible disease of the heart that many of us have and are too prideful to even see it!

What exactly is pride?

Note: I am only focusing on the selfish side of pride for this study. Taking pride in your work and accomplishments is not what I am talking about here. We are only discussing the sinful side of pride.

I looked it up in the dictionary and concordance and found things like:

> *A high or inordinate opinion of one's own dignity, importance, merit, or superiority, whether as cherished in the mind or as displayed in bearing, conduct, etc.; the state or feeling of being proud; a becoming or dignified sense of what is due to oneself or one's position or character; self-respect; self-esteem; pleasure or satisfaction taken in something done by or*

belonging to oneself or believed to reflect credit upon oneself;
pomp; swelling; loftiness and arrogance.

Simply Stated: *Pride is placing our own authority <u>above</u> God's. It is*
placing our plan, our greatness, and goodness ABOVE God's.

On the flip side: A very interesting fact is that the opposite of pride is
humility… but we'll get to that in a minute. Let's talk about pride a
little longer…

Pride means many things. However, the pride I am talking about says
the following…

I already know this

I don't have an issue with that

I am quite knowledgeable in spiritual matters

I read the Bible all the time

I know a lot

I am OK

I am spiritually aware enough to watch this program

I am not as bad off as so and so

My way is the right way

It's just…

It's only…

Pride also takes Scriptures and makes them fit our own selfish needs,
wants and desires.

Pride takes liberty in Christ and turns it into license to sin.

Pride takes itself far too seriously.

Pride cannot see other view points.

Pride thinks it knows it all and is unteachable.

Pride is <u>inward</u> oriented.

Being unteachable is <u>very</u> dangerous. If you are not teachable then you will never learn or be able to see sin crouching at the doorway of your heart. Pride is a gateway to the kind of sinful strongholds that may keep a person bound their entire lives.

Why?

Because they are so filled with this destructive mindset that they are completely blinded, and cannot see the muck they have gotten themselves in.

Something that may surprise you is that pride was originated from our adversary, satan. That fact alone makes me want to **humble myself** and rebuke pride before it even begins to creep into the recesses of my being. Read Isaiah 14:12-14 (the whole chapter if you can) to see how satan's pride is what got him booted out of the presence of the Almighty. *(Another reference tied in with Isaiah is; 1 Timothy 3:6)*

Be not wise in your own eyes; reverently fear and worship the Lord and turn entirely away from evil. – Proverbs 3:7

How do we keep pride far from us?

Humility

We must develop humility.

What is humility?

I looked it up in the dictionary and concordance and found things like:

The quality or condition of being humble; modest opinion or estimate of one's own importance, rank; mildness of disposition, gentleness of spirit; lowliness, meekness, submissiveness.

Simply stated: *Humility is meekness. It is free from pride and arrogance. Humility understands your flesh and inadequacies as a human being. It also understands that you do not know it all and that God is the one who should be behind the wheel and not us!*

Humility says the following…

> I do not know it all
>
> God is in control
>
> I need the Lord to even breathe properly
>
> I have much to learn

I can do all things THROUGH Christ Who gives me strength…it is NOT by my own doing. - Philippians 4:13

Humility understands that **God** is the giver, source and reason for strength, protection, knowledge, provision and ability. **Humility is submitted to the authority of Christ.** Humility understands that there is nothing great about oneself without the presence and help of the Lord. Humility is teachable and bendable to the will of God. Humility is always seeking more from God. Humility seeks peace and is able to lay down selfish needs and pride for the greater good in all relationships.

Humility is outward oriented.

Be careful to always be ready to do an honest self evaluation. Never assume you are mature in any area of your life to the extent that you do not need to learn. **We will never be perfected in any area of our lives until we are in Heaven.** There is always, always…ALWAYS room for growth. We must constantly be in learning, teachable and growing mode.

As soon as we think we know it all in any area of our lives, or feel like we are more knowledgeable than another with a different opinion: we need to get on our knees. That is the moment we need to make sure we are not only lined up with God's Word, but that we are acting in a **meek** and selfless manner.

Again, if you find yourself getting agitated and angry over a sermon or message, do not be so quick to write it off as nonsense. It could be good old fashioned conviction!

For whom the Lord loves He corrects, even as a father corrects the son in whom he delights. — Proverbs 3:12

For the Lord corrects and disciplines everyone whom He loves, and He punishes, even scourges, every son whom He accepts and welcomes to His heart and cherishes. — Hebrews 12:6

God loves you enough to let you know when you are in error! The Creator of the universe takes the time to make sure you KNOW the Truth!

Humble yourself and do not reject Him--and consequently become desensitized to the conviction of the Holy Spirit!

Be ever ready to seek God's face in the matter and be willing to hear what you may not want to hear. I can tell you from personal experience that more often than not, when we get annoyed or angry about a message, it is because of our own sin. We do not want to see it or even talk about it. We want to assume we know the answer and anyone who contradicts it, simply does not know as much as we do in the area. DANGER! **Humble yourself before the King and see what HE has to say!**

Humbleness is the opposite of pride.

Pride is a very destructive force in a person's life. There are several Scriptures I would like to showcase where wise Solomon explains the destructive power of pride…

When swelling and pride come, then emptiness and shame come also, but the **humble** *(those who are lowly, who have been pruned or chiseled by trial, and renounce self) are skillful and godly Wisdom and soundness. - Proverbs 11:2*

By pride and insolence comes only contention… - Proverbs 13:10

Pride goes before destruction and a haughty spirit before a fall. - Proverbs 16:18

A mans pride will bring him low, but he who is of a **humble** *spirit will obtain honor. - Proverbs 29:23*

When we develop a high opinion of ourselves and our abilities we are stepping into extremely dangerous territory. We must never allow ourselves to go there. **We must always remember that we are nothing without Christ.** Without Him we have no talents, happiness, comfort, joy, reason or Salvation--we have nothing. We may as well be dead without Him. **For with Him and in Him is where our**

strength and abilities come. Through Him we are able to withstand the evil attacks of the enemy. But, <u>without Him, we are NOTHING</u>.

Our Example was Meek

Take my yoke upon you, and learn of me: for I am **meek** *and lowly in heart: and ye shall find rest unto your souls. - Matthew 11:29*

Meek in this text means; gentle, **humble**, *mild, forbearing, and soothing.*

On the flip side; *prone to anger, soon angry, fierce, savage, irascible, perilous, and difficult.*

What a contrast! **Anger** is another sign of meekness being drowned out by the flesh. Very interesting…

The life that Jesus lived was an example of what a Christian's life should be. His character was above reproach. We can learn a LOT from the life that Jesus lived…

Meek…

This is a hard one for me. I am not meek by nature. It takes much effort for me to submit my character to God's Will in this area. I have been known to get angry very easily. However, with prayer, God's Word, and a daily laying down of the flesh, I have seen much improvement.

We all struggle with a lack of meekness on some level. We cannot ignore this though. We are called to be meek. Because **meekness is a fruit of the spirit**, it should become a natural part of our character <u>as we grow in Christ</u>.

Meek…gentle, humble, mild, forbearing, and soothing.

Let's submit our characters to God. Let's not be prone to or easily angered. Let us turn from fierce and savage behavior.

We will never be perfect.

However, <u>we can overcome this fleshly nature</u>. All God needs to work with is a **WILLING** vessel. If we humble ourselves before Him and repent, He will help us to become **meek**. He will help us become all that He created us to be!

Cease from anger and forsake wrath; fret not yourself–it tends only to evildoing. - Psalm 37:8

A self-confident fool utters all his anger, but a wise man holds it back and stills it. - Proverbs 29:11

A man of wrath stirs up strife, and a man given to anger commits and causes much transgression. - Proverbs 29:22

Blessed are the Meek...

Blessed are the meek, for they shall inherit the earth! – Matthew 5:5

Don't ever assume that you have "arrived" or that you are something more than you are. Yes, you are a child of the King of Kings, and yes you have authority and power over ALL evil. However, you are NOTHING without God and His Generous and Abounding Mercy!

As soon as we start getting caught up in "ourselves" and our own abilities, we are leaving God out of the equation and trying to be our own "mini versions" of God.

We must NEVER forget that it is He Who has made us...

*Know that the Lord is God! It is **He Who has made us**, not we ourselves [and we are His]! We are His people and the sheep of His pasture. – Psalm 100:3*

We must NEVER forget that it is He who gives us every good thing, talent, and all prosperity. He is our Source and He is Who gives us everything.

Whatever is good and perfect comes down to us from God our Father, Who created all the lights in the heavens. He never changes or casts a shifting shadow. - James 1:17

The most wonderful part of just acknowledging what is already true is that we are rewarded for it. God always has something wonderful for us when we are obedient.

We will be supremely blessed and happier when we **humble** ourselves to our Heavenly Father and give Him ALL the glory, honor and praise—not ourselves or our own abilities!

... He is the rewarder of those who earnestly and diligently seek Him. - Hebrews 11:6b

Meekness - Study Guide

Let's Pray:

Lord, please forgive me for allowing pride to ever visit my door. Thank You for loving me enough to tell me when I am doing, thinking or believing the wrong things. Help me to never think I know more than You. Help me to always be ready to learn and remain teachable in all things. Help me to hear You and accept Your correction. Help me to develop the fruit of meekness and to remove pride from my heart. I love You, Lord, and I want to always be in the Truth. I want to remain humble and lined up with Your Will for my life. Show me where there is sin and wrong thinking in my life, and help me to lay it down at Your feet. Thank You for the Truth and correction of Your Word. In Jesus' Mighty Name, Amen.

Memorize:

When swelling and pride come, then emptiness and shame come also, but with the humble (those who are lowly, who have been pruned or chiseled by trial, and renounce self) are skillful and godly Wisdom and soundness. - Proverbs 11:2

Dig Deeper:

If My people, who are called by My name, shall humble themselves, pray, seek, crave, and require of necessity My face and turn from their wicked ways, then will I hear from heaven, forgive their sin, and heal their land. - 2 Chronicles 7:14

These are very dark days. We must learn to humble ourselves before the Lord and let go of our selfish and earthly desires. There is MUCH more at stake here.

A man's pride will bring him low, but he who is of a humble spirit will obtain honor. - Proverbs 29:23

Pride will only destroy us. We will never find happiness with a pride filled heart.

Whoever will humble himself therefore and become like this little child [trusting, lowly, loving, forgiving] is greatest in the kingdom of heaven. - Matthew 18:4

This is a promise of God. If we will humble ourselves to God the way we expect our children to humble to us, we will be blessed for all eternity. Heaven is eternity. This is just the training ground. What we do here echoes in eternity.

Whoever exalts himself with haughtiness and empty pride shall be humbled (brought low), and whoever humbles himself [whoever has a modest opinion of himself and behaves accordingly] shall be raised to honor. - Matthew 23:12

There are good and bad outcomes to our actions. The Word gives us the pros and cons very clearly. This is a promise of the consequence of pride. We will be brought low. If we do not humble ourselves, we will BE humbled. That is not a pleasant thought!

But He gives us more and more grace. That is why He says, God sets Himself against the proud and haughty, but gives grace continually to the lowly. - James 4:6

When we humble ourselves we allow God the opportunity to grant us grace. When we fail, we need to go to God with a humble heart. Repent. He will give us grace. His Word says so. And, among MANY wonderful qualities God has, He NEVER lies.

Humbleness equals Grace given by God!

Scripture Study:

Look up the following Scriptures. I encourage you to really dig deep here and study them, look up any references and pray over them!

- Mark 7:20-23
- 1 Timothy 3:6
- 1 John 2:16
- Philippians 2:3
- Psalm 37:11
- Philippians 2:5-8
- 1 Peter 5:5
- Matthew 18:4
- Proverbs 11:2
- Romans 12:3
- Proverbs 3:34
- James 4:6
- Ephesians 4:2
- Psalm 147:6

Also, for an even deeper study, look up the following words in your concordance, and study the Scripture references: *meek, meekness, pride, humble, and humility.*

Fruit of Longsuffering

It is a fruit I live. Sometimes I feel like life is one long series of events that all lead to some form of suffering. Maybe I am alone in this thought process, however, I suspect that I am not. I hope that this book and my life testimony encourage all who read...

But the fruit of the Spirit is love, joy, peace, longsuffering, gentleness, goodness, faith, meekness, temperance: against such there is no law. And they that are Christ's have crucified the flesh with the affections and lusts. If we live in the Spirit, let us also walk in the Spirit. - Galatians 5:22-23

The original Greek word for **longsuffering** is **makrothumia** (mak-roth-oo-mee'-ah) and means, *forbearance, fortitude, patience, patiently.*

I want to look at the dictionary meanings for the following...

Patience - The bearing of provocation, annoyance, misfortune, or pain with out complaint, loss of temper, or anger. Quiet steady perseverance; even tempered.

Forbearance - Patient endurance, self control. An abstaining from the enforcement of a right.

Fortitude - Mental and emotional strength in facing adversity, danger, or temptation.

I don't know about you, but patience is <u>not</u> my strong point. However, I know that God gives us the ability to have and exercise it. We really can have patience when we ask for it. The problem is that we don't always realize that our answer requires us to "be" patient.

Let me explain…

We ask for patience.

So, God gives us lessons in patience through trials and adversity. The way to pass these lessons is to endure them without complaint. We must train ourselves to go *through* the storms not fight them. We cannot receive patience without the lessons. We must learn patience. Once we embrace that, we will see progress in the area of patience in our lives.

You must understand that we all already have the fruits of the spirit available to us. In order to see them **manifested** in our lives we must submit to God. In the case of *longsuffering,* we must embrace our difficulties and understand that they will only last a season and we *will* make it to the other side. They will also go much quicker if we go through them with patient endurance.

Remember the Israelites and how they took 40 years to take an 11 day trip?!

Why??

Murmuring and complaining…

Patience

Consider it wholly joyful, my brethren, whenever you are enveloped in or encounter trials of any sort or fall into various temptations.

Be assured and understand that the trial and proving of your faith bring out endurance and steadfastness and patience.

*But let endurance and steadfastness and patience have full play and do a thorough work, so that you may be people perfectly and fully developed with no defects, lacking in nothing. – **James 1:2-4***

We will start with the original Greek.

Joyful - chara (khar-ah'): *cheerfulness, calm delight, exceeding joy.*

Temptations - peirasmos (pi-ras-mos'): *a putting to proof, provocation, adversity, try.*

Proving - dokimion (dok-im'-ee-on): *a testing, trial, trustworthiness.*

Bring Out - katergazomai (kat-er-gad'-zom-ahee): *to work fully, accomplish, to finish.*

Patience (both verses) - **hupomone** (hoop-om-on-ay): *cheerful endurance, constancy.*

I think these verses are very interesting. Two things stood out the most for me, and they echo what I said in the last chapter…

One

In order to get the fruit of patience <u>we must go through trials</u>. The trials are what make us strong and help us to learn patience. The trials are like a training ground. You don't just get patience. You must earn it through experience and *endurance*.

Two

Not only do we have to go through the trials, but we must be calm and have a cheerful enduring attitude. As if the trial itself wasn't enough!

I don't know too many people that get excited over trials. The first thing that most of us do is ask God to take the trial away. Then we ask Him for patience. That is too funny. I think God has the best sense of humor. He truly is an AWESOME GOD!

What I believe James is trying to explain to us is that in this world we <u>will</u> have trials. There is no way out of it. It is part of life. I guess you can thank Adam and Eve for it. It is just the way it is. James is telling us that even though we must go through these trials, our Wonderful and Mighty God threw in a benefit.

The benefit is that when we go through these trials calmly, with a good attitude, and stand strong in our faith, we will become fully developed and lack nothing. Can you imagine lacking nothing?

I believe this means that we will be so focused on the victory and finding joy in the midst of the trials, that they will eventually have no affect on us. That is truly a wonderful gift from God...

Think about how fabulous it would be to get to a point in your walk that your emotions do not run amuck every time something goes wrong in your life--to get to a place where you have calmness and are cheerfully enduring.

WOW...I wish I could say I was at that place in my walk. Unfortunately, all I can tell you is that it is my goal. I want that kind of faith. I want to lose the emotional upheaval and gain the victorious calm.

Be patient, then, brothers, until the Lord's coming. See how the farmer waits for the land to yield its valuable crop and how patient he is for the autumn and spring rains. - James 5:7

Honestly, patience is something that I have struggled with for years. I want what I want and I want it <u>now</u>! I am certain that I am not the only one. We live in a society of impatience. We have minute rice, fast food restaurants, express check-out, speed dial, online stores, microwaves, and the list goes on and on and on. We all want it our way, right away.

God is not about speed. He has been around forever, since before time. He is in no hurry. When we ask Him for things, we expect our answers ASAP. And He takes His time. He does this to teach us to <u>trust</u> Him.

If we would just slow down and take the time to see people and hear their needs, then we may understand that life is not about "I want it now." It is about living our lives with purpose. It is about reaching out and shining light. It is about trusting our lives and everything about them to the One Who created time with only His Words. When we learn to do this we will have mastered patience….

However, I don't think we will ever give up that handy microwave.

Patience Through Trials

Blessed is the man who is patient under trial and stands up under temptation, for when he has stood the test and been approved, he will receive the victor's crown of life which God has promised to those who love Him. – James 1:12

Let's start with the original Greek text for blessed.

Blessed - **makarious** (mak-ar'-ee-os): *supremely blessed, fortunate, well off, happy.*

That sounds good to me! If I am patient and stand firm when I am tempted and under trials, I am blessed. However, it doesn't stop there-- I will also earn treasure in Heaven: *treasure that no thief can steal and no moth or rust can destroy.* It is a **promise** from God.

He wants to give us something we can have while we are here on earth. When we **stand firm** and remain patient under temptation and trial we become SUPREMELY blessed. We gain true happiness. Why? Because, we trust and are confident in our Mighty God and His Hand over our lives.

God also wants to give us an eternal reward for standing strong. He wants to give us a crown. YAY! I will wear mine proudly! I plan on getting that crown! I hope you do too.

Standing firm is an act of will. We must want to do it. It is never a matter of "can we?"... It is always a matter of "will we?"... God has given us the power to do all things. It is our job to receive that power and exercise it by faith.

But those who _wait_ on the Lord...

Have you not known? Have you not heard? The everlasting God, the LORD, The Creator of the ends of the earth, Neither faints nor is weary. His understanding is unsearchable. He gives power to the weak, And to those who have no might He increases strength. Even the youths shall faint and be weary, And the young men shall utterly fall, But those who wait on the LORD Shall renew their strength; They shall mount up with wings like eagles, They shall run and not be weary, They shall walk and not faint. - Isaiah 40:28-31

Isn't this an awesomely encouraging thing to know?? Our God... Indeed...OUR God, the Creator of the Universe does not grow weary. **He is always ready for battle and alert to all things.** He also gives us power as we wait on Him in confident trust.

AS we wait upon the Lord and trust Him THROUGH the trials and struggles, HE gives us <u>His</u> strength to endure and make it through. We will run...and NOT grow weary. We will walk...and NOT faint! YAY God!

But wait...

As with all of God's promises, there is something that must be done on our end.

Just like a good parent that rewards their children for doing right, our Heavenly Father, offers many promises for us, His children. One of them is strength. Not just any strength either...<u>continually RENEWED strength</u>.

What do we have to do to get it??

WAIT and TRUST.

Yes, trials WILL come. Yes, we may have to walk through fire and dark valleys. However, we will have the strength of the Almighty,

Great I Am WITH us through all of it AS WE WAIT upon Him and TRUST Him in the midst of them.

We are assured and know that all things work together and are fitting into a plan for good to and for those who love God and are called according to His design and purpose. For those whom He foreknew, He also destined from the beginning to be molded into the image of His Son that He might become the firstborn among many brethren. And those whom He thus foreordained, He also called; and those whom He called, He also justified (putting them into right standing with Himself). And those whom He justified, He also glorified. What then shall we say to [all] this? If God is for us, who can be against us? [Who can be our foe, if God is on our side?] - Romans 8:28-31

There is a purpose for everything we must endure. God is not surprised by our struggles, problems, and issues of life. He is <u>never</u> caught off guard. Even when we choose to step out of His Will and come back, He has an alternate plan for our good. **He is always molding us and working things out for His purpose and our good.** He has our backs and will never leave us or forsake us…no matter what. He loves us and is only looking out for our best interest.

Even the most painful things in life have a purpose. You see, God never promised a life without pain. Salvation does not mean a trouble-free life. Pain has a purpose: **Pain brings us to our knees and helps us to see the glory of His Name.** Pain hurts our fleshly person. However, pain must occur for us to become the beautiful masterpiece that the Potter is designing. Parts of the molding process can sometimes go unnoticed or without any real consideration on our parts. Yet, when we feel the burn of the kiln, we sure do want to buckle, eh?

We must not allow ourselves to get so caught up in the issues of life that we forget what God's Word says about them…

AS we wait and trust, we WILL gain strength

And

ALL things…

Not some…

ALL *things work together and are fitting into a plan for good to and for those who love God and are called according to His design and purpose. – Romans 8:28*

More on the Art of Waiting

As I mentioned earlier, patience is not my strong suit and I am most certainly <u>not</u> a fan of waiting. I will do everything in my power to avoid waiting. I choose the shortest lines, avoid traffic at all costs, look for quickest ways to perform tasks, etc. If there is a way to shorten the wait, I will find it, do it, and make it happen. I hate waiting.

Unfortunately, waiting is part of life:

We must wait for our pay checks—even though the work has already been done.

We must wait for things to cook.

We must wait for our favorite show's new episodes.

We must wait in lines.

We must wait for take out.

We must wait for traffic lights.

A parent must wait 10 months to hold their precious baby for the first time.

We must wait for many things.

And, we must wait on the Lord.

There is no avoiding waiting.

But those who wait on the LORD Shall renew their strength; They shall mount up with wings like eagles, They shall run and not be weary, They shall walk and not faint. - Isaiah 40:31

Waiting is a part of our walk with the Lord. He is not a genie in a bottle that pops out when we rub on the side of it. He does not come when we fret over the difficulties of life. He will come and He will do when <u>HE</u> is ready--in HIS perfect timing. It is OUR job to wait on Him and TRUST Him. You see, in regards to waiting on the Lord, it requires trusting Him:

> Trusting that He will come through for us as He has in the past.
>
> AND
>
> Trusting that He knows best and that His timing is better than our own.

He is always doing little things to teach me, and waiting is one that this hard headed woman fights every step of the way. I know that when my computer crashed awhile ago and I had to wait a month for Him to provide the money to fix it, He was teaching me. I had to rely on Him for the patience of my subscribers and those who paid for something they were being forced to wait for. Yet, He came through and each person was very kind and patient with me. I am SO very thankful that the Lord loves me enough to make me wait!

What a bunch of spoiled brats we would be if we never had to wait for anything!?

I wait for the Lord, I expectantly wait, and in His word do I hope. - Psalm 130:5

Waiting on the Lord is for OUR benefit:

It builds hope.

It helps us trust Him more.

It builds our faith.

It helps us rely on His strength rather than our own.

It teaches us obedience and patience.

Waiting is a good thing.

Do I like waiting after writing this devotional?

Um…

No.

However, I love my Daddy God and if HE says waiting is for my own good and that it is required, then I will learn to cultivate the fruit of patience in my life through waiting on Him. I will choose to trust Him and allow Him to teach me as I wait in line, traffic and for Him to move in the areas I desire. Why? Because NO ONE loves me like He does. No one cares for me as intimately and profoundly as He does-- no one. I will wait because I know He loves me and would never do anything to harm me. I will trust Him and praise Him as I wait…

I WAITED patiently and expectantly for the Lord; and He inclined to me and heard my cry. - Psalm 40:1

Suffering...

As I conclude this hard topic of longsuffering, I am compelled to share that I am nowhere near the place I want to be in this area. I suffer a lot. Please do not misunderstand, we all have problems and I am not trying to cry the blues or even suggest that my problems are bigger than another. What I am trying to share is that looking at my own life, just me... I see a long, tedious and sometimes bordering on unbearable series of events that leave me with deep set scars that never fully heal.

I find life to be very hard and try desperately to search for the good, and of course, when I do, I find it.

However...

The suffering aspect of longsuffering is what makes life difficult through the lenses of MY eyes. I cry out to the Lord and beg Him to allow just one aspect of my existence to be easier. Then there are days when I yell out to Him and want to know WHY He chose to allow Me to have to be the one with the story that relates to so many? Why did I have to start my suffering as young as infancy? Why?

To reach you?

Maybe.

I wish I could say I found comfort in reaching others though the pains and trials of my own experiences...Sadly, I cannot. All I can say is that I hope that my life means something and that the pain, wounds, tears and craziness of my existence on this planet is worth more than words on a page.

I pray that I not only reach people, but I inspire them to press on, seek God more and to endure to the finish line! I also pray that my transparency frees me and helps me to reach that same finish line!

Finally, I want to encourage you by letting you know that you are not alone! Life is hard and we are all walking our own long hard roads! I also want to remind you that our God is not a liar and that He WILL complete all the work that He started in each of us!

And I am certain that God, who began the good work within you, will continue His work until it is finally finished on the day when Christ Jesus returns. - Philippians 1:6

Longsuffering - Study Guide

Let's Pray:

Lord, thank You for loving me enough to allow me to be perfected through the molding process of fire. Thank You for having a perfect plan and purpose for my life even if I do not always understand it. Help me to see Your hand in everything. Help me to overcome the trials and pains of this life. Help me to rely on You and reach out for YOUR strength. Help me to cultivate the fruit of longsuffering. THANK YOU for making it available to me as I wait on You and trust you through my struggles. I love You, Daddy. Thank You for loving me. In Jesus' Mighty Name, Amen.

Memorize:

Trust in the Lord with all your heart; do not depend on your own understanding. - Proverbs 3:5

Dig Deeper:

Have you not known? Have you not heard? The everlasting God, the LORD, The Creator of the ends of the earth, Neither faints nor is weary. His understanding is unsearchable. He gives power to the weak, And to those who have no might He increases strength. Even the youths shall faint and be weary, And the young men shall utterly fall, But those who wait on the LORD Shall renew their strength; They shall mount up with wings like eagles, They shall run and not be weary, They shall walk and not faint. - Isaiah 40:28-31 (NKJV)

Isn't this an awesomely encouraging thing to know?? Our God... Indeed... OUR God, the Creator of the Universe does not grow weary. He is always ready for battle and alert to all things. He also gives us power to be patient--as we wait on Him in confident trust.

As we wait upon the Lord and trust Him through the trials and struggles of this life, He gives us His strength to endure and make it through. He helps us cultivate the fruit of longsuffering.

But wait…

As with all of God's promises, there is something that must be done on our end.

Just like a good parent rewards their children for doing right, Daddy God, offers many promises for His children. One of them is strength. Not just any strength either: continually renewed strength.

What do we have to do to get it??

Be patient and TRUST Him.

Yes, trials WILL come. Yes, we may have to walk through fire and dark valleys. However, we will have the strength of the Almighty, Great I Am, with us through all of it as we wait upon Him and TRUST Him in the midst of them.

We are assured and know that all things work together and are fitting into a plan for good to and for those who love God and are called according to His design and purpose. For those whom He foreknew, He also destined from the beginning to be molded into the image of His Son, that He might become the firstborn among many brethren. And those whom He thus foreordained, He also called; and those whom He called, He also justified (putting them into right standing with Himself). And those whom He justified, He also glorified. What then shall we say to [all] this? If God is for us, who [can be] against us? [Who can be our foe, if God is on our side?] - Romans 8:28-31

There is a purpose for everything we must endure. God is not surprised by our struggles, problems, and issues of life. He is never caught off guard. Even when we choose to step out of His Will and come back, He has an alternate plan for our good. He is always molding us and working things out for His purpose and our good. He has our backs and will never, ever, *ever*, leave us or forsake us…no matter what. He loves us and is only looking out for our best interest.

Even the most painful things in life have a purpose.

Pain brings us to our knees and helps us to see the glory of His Name. Pain hurts our fleshly person. However, pain must occur for us to become the beautiful masterpiece that the Potter is designing. Parts of the molding process can sometimes go unnoticed or without any real consideration on our parts. Yet, when we feel the burn of the kiln, we sure do want to buckle, eh?

In closing, let us not allow ourselves to get so caught up in the issues of life that we forget what God's Word says about them…

As we wait and trust (develop the fruit of longsuffering--aka patience), we WILL gain strength and all things… not some… <u>ALL things work together and are fitting into a plan for good to and for those who love God and are called according to His design and purpose.</u>

Scripture Study:

Look up the following Scriptures. I encourage you to really dig deep here and study them, look up any references and pray over them!

- James 5:11
- Romans 12:12
- Psalm 37:7-9
- Psalm 46:1-3
- Philippians 4:13
- Psalm 40:4
- Psalm 55:22
- Isaiah 41:10

- Galatians 6:9
- Philippians 4:6
- Psalm 56:3-4
- Micah 7:7

Also, for an even deeper study, look up the following words in your concordance: *steadfast, patience, longsuffering, trust the Lord, wait on the Lord,* and study the Scripture references.

Fruit of Joy

I have been told that I have the fruit of joy welling up inside me. Unfortunately, I do not see it and found this to be my most challenging fruit to write about—so far…Simply because I do not see joy evident in my heart and mind. I want to see it manifested in my life.

When I think of joy, I think of freedom, happiness, laughter and a carefree spirit. I do not see this in my own walk. However, I want to! So, join me on the journey to finding joy…

But the fruit of the Spirit is love, joy, peace, longsuffering, gentleness, goodness, faith, meekness, temperance: against such there is no law. And they that are Christ's have crucified the flesh with the affections and lusts. If we live in the Spirit, let us also walk in the Spirit. - Galatians 5:22-23

The original Greek word for joy is **chara** (khar-ah) and is used 59 times in the New Testament. It means: *cheerfulness, calm delight, gladness, be exceedingly joyful.*

This tells me that Christians should not be walking around with sour looks on their faces and having bad attitudes. We should be happy and joyful. People should want what we have. They should see our lights shining through our attitude and smiles. I understand that we all have problems and sometimes very bad days…but being upset and angry about it isn't going to make it better. It will only make us more upset and magnify the problem.

Proverbs 15:13 says, A glad heart makes a cheerful countenance, but by sorrow of heart the spirit is broken.

Our attitudes can determine how long we go through a trial. Think about the Israelites. If they spent more time being thankful and happy to be out of Egypt, instead of murmuring and complaining, they would have been able to see the Promised Land. Sadly, none of them did....only their children were able to experience that promise.

Proverbs 17:22 says, a happy heart is good medicine and a cheerful mind works healing, but a broken spirit dries up the bones.

Just by having a good attitude and being of good cheer we bring health and healing to our bodies. However, when we allow our anger, disappointments and bad attitudes to rule us, we bring sickness, sadness and disease into our lives.

So, when troubles come, be of good cheer. Nothing is that bad. That's right, I said **nothing**. No matter what you lose or what you go through, nothing is worse than an eternity in hell. Knowing that you are going to be with Jesus when you die should make you happy for the rest of your life. You are chosen of God. You are His child and He adores you.

Don't get mad, get glad. You can choose to make your life better simply by changing your attitude. No matter what we go through…if we keep a cheerful heart and positive attitude, we can make it through. And it will be a whole lot easier than being angry and sick about it.

If you don't think that you can be positive, then, start focusing on all you have to be thankful for. Your health, family, spouse, clean water, Salvation, roof over your head…

Count your blessings not your sorrows.

Beyond Definition

We proclaim to you the One who existed from the beginning, whom we have heard and seen. We saw Him with our own eyes and touched Him with our own hands. He is the Word of life.

This one who is life itself was revealed to us, and we have seen Him. And now we testify and proclaim to you that He is the one who is eternal life. He was with the Father, and then He was revealed to us.

We proclaim to you what we ourselves have actually seen and heard so that you may have fellowship with us. And our fellowship is with the Father and with his Son, Jesus Christ.

*We are writing these things so that you may **fully share our <u>joy</u>**.*

This is the message we heard from Jesus and now declare to you: God is light, and there is no darkness in Him at all.

So we are lying if we say we have fellowship with God but go on living in spiritual darkness; we are not practicing the truth.

But if we are living in the light, as God is in the light, then we have fellowship with each other, and the blood of Jesus, His Son, cleanses us from all sin.

If we claim we have no sin, we are only fooling ourselves and not living in the truth.

But if we confess our sins to Him, He is faithful and just to forgive us our sins and to cleanse us from all wickedness.

If we claim we have not sinned, we are calling God a liar and showing that His word has no place in our hearts. - 1 John 1

1 John 1 is a short chapter, however, I believe that we are seeing the Biblical definition of the **chara** (khar-ah) **joy** that God is trying to impart on each of us.

You see, there is a great joy in knowing that you are loved and forgiven by the Creator of all things. There is an unmatched joy in the knowledge that the King of Kings and Lord of Lords cared enough about each of us to send His only and blameless Son to pay the price that WE deserved.

The **chara** (khar-ah) Joy is so much more than any definition can offer. It is a joy that comes straight from Heaven. It is a joy that encompasses our King, and that He shares with each of us—if we let Him.

Imagine giving a gift to someone you love and they throw it back in your face…

Joy is a gift from your King…

Receive it.

Joy of the Lord is Our Strength

And be not grieved and depressed, for the joy of the Lord is your strength and stronghold. - Nehemiah 8:10b

Let's face it, life is hard. It is filled with trials, sadness, and pain. There is no escape from the fact that sin is in the world, and with it will come joy-robbers.

However, in the midst of all the pain, sorrow and trials of life is strength—the kind of strength that comes straight from the Father into our hearts. Our hearts must be willing though. God will not force Himself on us. He is a perfect gentleman. We must be <u>willing</u> to receive the strength of His joy.

If we allow Him to work in our hearts, trust Him and walk with Him through this crazy life, we will receive the gift of His joy. He will develop the fruit of joy in our hearts and we will be stronger. We will have His strength abiding in our hearts and mind.

Think about this for a minute…

The very nature of God is joyful.

God… the Living God… the All Knowing King of All… the Great I AM takes His Joy and places it in us. Through it we have strength to endure anything and everything life throws at us!

Joy in Unity

*Fill up and complete my **joy** by living in harmony and being of the same mind and one in purpose, having the same love, being in full accord and of one harmonious mind and intention. - Philippians 2:2*

I encourage you to read the entire chapter.

When we are esteeming others, keeping our motives pure and walking in unity, we <u>will be</u> filled with joy!

As I mulled this over, I could see how this makes perfect sense. Think about how it feels when you are in a disagreement with someone…

We are angry, bitter, stressed out and out of right relationship. I also believe on some level we are harboring unforgiveness.

What leads to strife and how do conflicts, quarrels, and fighting originate among you? - James 4:1a

Conflict means; in opposition, clash, disagree, strife, controversy, quarrel, collision.

The opposite of conflict is; reconcile, peace, truce.

Conflicts almost always begin because someone either does not get their way, someone gets offended, or people do not agree about something. Many times, we just don't want to let things go, we don't want to give something up, or we are just plain stubborn. When the Church allows quarrels and conflict to go unchecked, it weakens us as a whole. That is why our adversary works overtime trying to generate discord in the Body.

He wants to split us up, cause us to magnify the faults in others, place unrealistic expectations on leaders and those we respect, destroy the Church with pride and discord, and try to make us act out in a sinful way.

The only way we can overcome this is to recognize it, and then not allow it to manifest itself in us, therefore disabling the Church. Until we get over ourselves and start loving each other and being obedient children of God, we will continue to see the Church become more and more powerless.

James goes so far as to say that when we hate, it is like we are committing murder in our hearts. That statement sounds a lot like when Jesus said that by simply looking at another with lust, we have already committed adultery. These are HUGE statements.

It is an issue that begins on the inside. It is a heart matter. And where does it all begin?

Our thought life.

Our minds are the first line of attack. The enemy sends all his forces to our minds, because he knows that if he can get into our thoughts, he will get our hearts.

We must remember…

Discord takes away joy.

Lack of unity kills joy.

If we allow God to work in us, forgive others, let go of strife, and never allow conflict to rise up in our hearts to the point of quarrelsome bitter refutes--joy will be within our reach.

Unforgiveness Hinders Joy

For if you forgive men when they sin against you, your heavenly Father will also forgive you. But if you do not forgive men their sins, your Father will not forgive your sins. - Matthew 6:14-15

Unforgiveness means; unrelenting, unyielding, not allowing for carelessness or weakness, blame, condemn, charge.

The opposite of unforgiveness is; forgive, pardon, excuse, reprieve, cease to feel resentment.

This is one of those Scriptures we like to bypass. We don't like to spend too much time examining it. It makes us very uncomfortable. We all have had our share of forgiveness battles. We have all been wronged on some level… some more than others.

We seem to like hanging onto our anger and unforgiveness. We even make excuses for holding onto them. Unfortunately, none of our reasonings can change the infallible, uncompromising, authoritive Word of Almighty God. Jesus makes it crystal clear: *Forgive and be forgiven. Do not forgive and you will not be forgiven.*

It's more than John 3:16 and 1John 1:9, friends. It's about being obedient and giving the same as we hope to receive. Why should we be pardoned if we will not pardon another's offense? We must take the words of Jesus VERY seriously. We must develop a forgiving heart and release our hurts and anger to Him. We must learn to obey this command. If we do not, then we are playing a game that does not have a happy ending.

Harboring unforgiveness is a surefire way to remove joy from your life.

Unforgiveness is a bitter root that will inevitably destroy our hearts and prevent good fruit from developing in our lives.

Unforgiveness will lead us away from God, away from joy and away from our own forgiveness!

Then Peter came to him and asked, "Lord, how often should I forgive someone who sins against me? Seven times?"

"No, not seven times," Jesus replied, "but seventy times seven!"

"Therefore, the Kingdom of Heaven can be compared to a king who decided to bring his accounts up to date with servants who had borrowed money from him.

In the process, one of his debtors was brought in who owed him millions of dollars.

He couldn't pay, so his master ordered that he be sold—along with his wife, his children, and everything he owned—to pay the debt.

"But the man fell down before his master and begged him, 'Please, be patient with me, and I will pay it all.'

Then his master was filled with pity for him, and he released him and forgave his debt.

"But when the man left the king, he went to a fellow servant who owed him a few thousand dollars. He grabbed him by the throat and demanded instant payment.

"His fellow servant fell down before him and begged for a little more time. 'Be patient with me, and I will pay it,' he pleaded.

But his creditor wouldn't wait. He had the man arrested and put in prison until the debt could be paid in full.

"When some of the other servants saw this, they were very upset. They went to the king and told him everything that had happened.

Then the king called in the man he had forgiven and said, 'You evil servant! I forgave you that tremendous debt because you pleaded with me.

Shouldn't you have mercy on your fellow servant, just as I had mercy on you?'

Then the angry king sent the man to prison to be tortured until he had paid his entire debt.

"That's what my heavenly Father will do to you if you refuse to forgive your brothers and sisters from your heart." - Matthew 18:21-35

Peter asked a valid question. I mean, I can almost hear him… "When is enough…enough??"

Thankfully, Jesus makes it very clear how important forgiveness is. He does not mince words. There should be no limit to how many times we forgive. We must forgive or we will <u>not</u> be forgiven. Period.

But if you do not forgive men their sins, your Father will not forgive your sins... - Matthew 6:15

Neither Consider Things of Old...

Do not remember the former things; neither <u>consider</u> the things of old.

Behold, I am doing a <u>new</u> thing! Now, it springs forth; do you not know it and will you not give heed to it? I will even make a way in the wilderness and <u>rivers</u> in the desert. - Isaiah 43:18-19

Let's take a deeper look into the meanings of some of these words.

The original Hebrew word for **consider** is **biyn** (bene) and means; *to separate mentally. This means ignore, overlook, and disregard.*

New – chadash (khaw-dawsh'): fresh, new thing, to rebuild, renew. I also looked this up in the thesaurus and found; restore, fix, repair, and reconstruct!

Rivers – nahar (naw-har') or nehar (neh-har'): to sparkle, be cheerful, to flow, be lightened. According to the Webster's dictionary and thesaurus, lightened means; to make lighter the weight, to lessen the load, to make less burdensome, to cheer or gladden, perk up, revive, and uplift.

Now, let's reread the Scriptures using these meanings.

Ignore and disregard yesterday.

Behold, I am doing a fresh thing, I am rebuilding, fixing, and restoring you. Now, it springs forth; do you not know it and will you not give heed to it? I will even make a way in the wilderness and revive you and lighten your burdens.

What an amazing God we serve! There is none like Him. I am in awe of all the many ways He blesses us. He has already done so much for each of us. Thankfully, He is never quite done… He also wants to restore us and bring forth newness…

He Makes ALL Things New! - Revelation 21:5

We need to get over yesterday and step into the spring of today--the newness of each day. Every day is a new beginning. Every day is a chance to be better than the day before.

That's not even the best part! The best part is that He... yes... our Beloved and Loving God makes it all new!

He fixes us!

He restores us!

He heals us!

He rebuilds what others have torn down!

He lightens our burdens!

He uplifts us!

He makes us glad!

We just need to allow Him to do His job!

His Word tells us that He does all this for us. So, when we have bad days... have been hurt... failed miserably... remember...

He makes ALL things new... not some: ALL.

I do not believe that we even have to wait for a new day to come! Every minute is new. Every second before is things of OLD! Live each minute in the NEW!

Let God restore you and gladden your heart. You are not alone. Your Father in Heaven is waiting with open arms to make all… not some… **all things new** in your life!!

WHOO HOO!

I could dance right now! Couldn't you??? I mean WOW! As if He has not done enough… He wants every minute of our lives new… fresh… glad… and filled with hope, restoration, and JOY!

Joy - Study Guide

Let's Pray:

Lord, thank You for all You have given me. Thank You for the gift of Salvation. Help me to see all the wonderful things in my life and not focus on the negative. Help me to have a positive attitude during difficult seasons in my life. Help me to remember all that is good in my life. Help me to develop joy in my life and to attract others to You through the joy that overflows from my heart. Thank You. In Jesus' Mighty Name, Amen.

Memorize:

And now, dear brothers and sisters, one final thing. Fix your thoughts on what is true, and honorable, and right, and pure, and lovely, and admirable. Think about things that are excellent and worthy of praise. - Philippians 4:8

Dig Deeper:

Life can feel so defeating sometimes. It can be hard to even think about being happy or joy-filled, let alone developing the fruit of joy! Below you will find several reasons to not only be be joy-filled, but also give you strength and victory on the journey!!

Note: I would like to encourage you to look up the Scripture references for all of them and check them in different translations as well. Be encouraged and GLAD that YOU are a child of the Most High!

God makes all grace and favor come to me. (ref. 2 Corinthians 9:8)

I love when the word ALL is used in a Scripture! ALL grace and favor will come to me! All.

I am the handiwork of God. Recreated in Christ Jesus. (ref. Ephesians 2:10)

The Creator of the Universe knit me in my Mother's womb. I am HIS handiwork and have been made new through the Blood of Christ! :D

When I get close to God...He gets close to me. (ref. James 4:8)

You see, God never leaves. He remains in the same place we left Him. So, when WE get close to Him, He is able to be closer to us! Why do we even leave His side??

Greater is He that is in me than he that is in the world. (ref. 1 John 4:4)

The battle has already been won! The enemy IS defeated! If we could grasp this, we would see more victory in our lives. BELIEVE!

God has a plan...a GOOD plan for my life! (ref. Jeremiah 29:11)

His plan is FAR better than anything we could dream up! Trust Him!

God WILL finish what He started! (ref. Philippians 1:6)

Our God does not have half finished projects. He ALWAYS finishes what He starts. HE WILL complete what He started in us!

I am a NEW Creation! The old is GONE! (ref. 2 Corinthians 5:17)

I am NO LONGER the woman I was! I am a NEW creation! I am the handiwork of God and when I fail, instead of beating myself up, I need to pick myself up, dust off my bottom and remember that I am NEW!

My needs WILL be met! (ref. Philippians 4:19)

God will take care of me and meet my needs. If He says it, He will do it!

God will NEVER leave me or forsake me! (ref. Hebrews 13:5)

I LOVE this one! My Daddy God will never, never, never leave me!!!

His abundant mercy saved me!! (ref. Titus 3:4-5)

Thank YOU, Lord for MERCY! Thank You, Jesus for dying for unworthy me!

My Savior walked a mile in my shoes! He understands my weaknesses! (ref. Hebrews 4:15-16)

This is one of the greatest things to know! Jesus did not only leave the comforts of Heaven to fulfill a purpose of Salvation for US…He ALSO walked far more than a MILE in our shoes! He lived a common life with no frills and was tempted just as we are! He overcame FOR us and made a way so that we can ALSO be over comers!

I am the head and not the tail. I am above and not beneath. (ref. Deuteronomy 28:13)

What more can I add to this one???

No weapon formed against me shall prosper. (ref. Isaiah 54:17)

No… not one… NO… NO… NO weapon formed against us shall prosper. PERIOD!

Jesus overcame the world and its distresses for me. (ref. John 16:31)

He already paid the price!

NOTHING can separate me from God's love! (ref. Romans 8:38)

Nothing. Not one thing. God loves each of us so profoundly and abundantly. All we must do is receive and believe!

Scripture Study:

Look up the following Scriptures. I encourage you to really dig deep here and study them, look up any references and pray over them!

- Psalm 118:24

- Matthew 6:14-15

- Ephesians 4:31-32

- James 1:2-4

- Philippians 4:4

- 1 Peter 5:7

- Proverbs 17:22

- James 5:13

- Psalm 16:11

- Romans 15:13

- Psalm 126:3

- Proverbs 15:13

- Psalms 91 (whole chapter)

- Psalms 119:75-76

- Revelation 21:10-27 (be encouraged by the description of your final destination! Yay!)

Also, for an even deeper study, look up the following words in your concordance: *joy, forgive unforgiveness, glad, happy, joy of the Lord,* and study the Scripture references.

Fruit of Goodness

When I set out to do this portion of the Fruit of the Spirit study, I thought I would have a hard time trying to find what goodness would mean as far as fruit in our lives.

However, as usual, God never ceases to amaze me! He showed me so many aspects of goodness and what it means for us, His children. Let me share what was revealed...

But the fruit of the Spirit is love, joy, peace, longsuffering, gentleness, goodness, faith, meekness, temperance: against such there is no law. And they that are Christ's have crucified the flesh with the affections and lusts. If we live in the Spirit, let us also walk in the Spirit. - Galatians 5:22-23

GOODNESS

Let's start with the Greek meaning and then use the dictionary.

Goodness – agathosune (ag-ath-o-soo'-nay): *beneficence.*

Beneficent means: *doing good or causing good to be done; charitable.*

Charitable means: *generous in gifts to aid the indigent, ill, homeless, etc. Kindly or lenient in judging people.* (we will look at the last part of "charitable" more in the next chapter!)

Doing good or causing good to be done...

This is something that can bring much joy to not only us, but for others as well. Simple acts of kindness are a nice way to show goodness. Here are some ideas to get you started--but don't stop with these. By all means come up with your own. The important thing to learn here is to do kind things and show goodness as often as possible.

Goodness Expressed:

Smile

Buy a person or family their food anonymously when you're eating out at a restaurant.

Bring your cart back inside when you're finished at the grocery store.

When you see something out of place while shopping, take the time to put it back.

Help sponsor missions trips.

Give a bigger tip when the service is bad.

Offer to help an elderly person when you see them struggling.

Give when you see a need instead of ignoring it.

Open the door for someone.

Give a compliment.

Say thank you.

Pay the electric bill of someone you know would benefit from it.

Pay someone's rent or mortgage.

Clean your area up when you go out to eat.

Visit a nursing home.

Give a gift certificate to that nice cashier you see every week.

Listen… I mean really listen.

Mow your neighbor's grass.

Call someone you never call.

Write someone you care for that lives far away.

Give to that beggar on the corner that you see.

Or better yet, go buy him a meal. You will never forget the gratitude in his eyes. I promise.

Pay for the toll of the person behind you. (You can do this for a fast food drive-through too!)

Instead of trying to get money for those old clothes, give them to the needy.

Sponsor a needy child at Christmas. (I was one of them and some person made my Christmas that year. I would have gotten nothing.)

Tell someone your sorry… first.

Goodness for You… Yeah You:

Get a hobby and spend at least two hours a week doing it with no kids or spouse (if you have them)--just you or a group that is doing the same hobby.

Take a long, hot bath/shower.

Take a walk by yourself once in a while.

Join a fitness club and take care of your temple.

Pray

When you have a little extra money don't always be so practical. It's OK to buy yourself something once in a while.

Smile, you'll age better.

Laugh more, you'll stay healthy.

Put some money aside each week for something that will make you happy... hobby, new game for your game system, trip, new golf clubs, a dress, whatever makes you happy and is good.

Give yourself a break! I mean think about it... you are LOVED by the Creator of the Universe!!!

Sowing and Reaping Judgment

Let's look at the second part of **charitable** from the previous chapter...

Just in case you need a reminder: charitable means: *generous in gifts to aid the indigent, ill, homeless, etc. Kindly or lenient in judging people.*

I think it is important that we all are very careful in how we view others. It is very easy to get on our spiritual "high horse" and make judgments about another. We must be very careful. Remember what the Word says about judging... judge not lest ye be judged... If you sow judgment you will reap judgment.

Let me give you an example...

You read an article about some horrible thing that one person did to another person or people. Right away you think and/or perhaps say, *"What is wrong with that person? They should get the death penalty... I think they should rot in prison...They should burn in hell..."* I'm sure you get my meaning.

Who are you or me to decide those things? **We are not God.** We do not know a person's heart. We cannot assume anything. Sin is sin. You and I are no better. However, we have the Blood of Jesus over us and they do not. The first thing that we should be thinking and saying to our friends is: *"Let's pray for this situation."* We need to pray not only for the victims, but for the one who did the deed as well.

It does not matter what the crime or offense is. Our job is <u>NEVER</u> to judge. That is God's job and **only** His job. <u>Our job is to pray, speak life over the situation, pray, keep our opinions to ourselves, pray, and have compassion for all involved.</u> After all, we are talking about souls here--something that is very precious to God and very much coveted by satan.

Anyway, the next time you encounter an unusual situation or read a horrific headline, think twice before you open your mouth in any kind of judgment. Be VERY careful what you sow.

Let's dig deeper into this and look at mercy...

Blessed are the Merciful

Blessed are the merciful, for they will be shown mercy. - Matthew 5:7

The Webster's dictionary definition of mercy is: compassionate or kindly forbearance shown toward an offender or enemy. An act of kindness, compassion, or favor.

Ever been deeply wounded by someone?

I once saw a story on a nightly news program. It was about a Christian woman whose young daughter was kidnapped and killed by a very sick man. She went a whole year wondering if her daughter was even alive. Then on the anniversary of her daughter's disappearance she received a phone call from the offender and later found out he killed her baby girl.

How would you react?

Would you hate this man?

Would you be able to forgive and show him mercy?

Honestly, I am not sure that I could--especially to the extent that this woman did…

This godly woman prayed for that man every day. She forgave him and became his pen pal! She visited him in prison, and came to actually care for him in a parental way. She chose to let the horrible and unthinkable thing that he did go. And she forgave as she had been forgiven. This precious woman showed the kind of compassion and mercy that Jesus lived out for you and me.

You see, in God's eyes we have all fallen short. No one is better than another. We are ALL sinners until we repent and receive the

Blood of Jesus. God showed us ALL mercy when He sent His Only Son to die for us. Jesus showed us ALL mercy when He died on the cross for our sins. Not one of us should ever forget the VERY high cost of our Salvation.

Now, the next time your husband forgets a special day… or your wife speaks rudely to you… or when a co-worker talks about you behind your back… or any offense occurs in your life--big or small…

Remember the woman I mentioned earlier and how she was able to overcome. Remember all that your Father in Heaven has done for you. Remember the mercy that He shows you each and every day of your life.

Then, you will experience the kind of goodness that the Holy Spirit living in you manifests in your life.

Forgiveness

In order to show mercy and release someone from an offense, we must forgive them. It is the ONLY way.

For if you forgive men when they sin against you, your heavenly Father will also forgive you.

But if you do not forgive men their sins, your Father will not forgive your sins. - Matthew 6:14-15

These are pretty scary words. You would think this would be enough to make us forgive...

This is one of those Scriptures we like to bypass. We don't like to spend too much time examining it. It makes us very uncomfortable. We all have had our share of forgiveness battles. We have all been wronged on some level....some more than others.

We seem to have this need to hold onto our anger and unforgiveness. We even make excuses for ourselves. Unfortunately, none of our reasonings can change the infallible Word of the Living God. Jesus makes it crystal clear: Forgive and be forgiven. Do not forgive and you will not be forgiven.

It's more than John 3:16 and 1John 1:9, dear friends. It is about being obedient and giving the same as we are seeking. Why should we be pardoned if we will not pardon an offense? Well, we will not. We must take the words of Christ VERY seriously. We must develop a forgiving heart and release our hurts and anger to the Lord. We must obey this command. If we do not, then we are playing a game that does not have a happy ending.

Luke 6:37b - Acquit and forgive and release (give up resentment, let it drop), and you will be acquitted and forgiven and released.

This is classic sewing and reaping. Forgive, and be forgiven. You give, you get.

Ephesians 4:31-32 - Let all bitterness and indignation and wrath and resentment and quarreling and slander be banished from you. And become useful and helpful and kind to one another, tenderhearted, forgiving one another readily and freely, as God in Christ forgave you.

Colossians 3:13 - Be gentle and forbearing with one another and, if one has a difference (a grievance or complaint) against another, readily pardoning each other; even as the Lord has freely forgiven you, so you must also forgive.

It is very clear that we must remember… we have been *forgiven* many sins. It is very clear that we must **forgive** others who have wronged us in any way. It is very clear that if we do not forgive…we will not be forgiven. This is a very important thing to keep in mind. We cannot walk around thinking that we will stroll into Heaven when we've harbored *unforgiveness* in our hearts. These are not my words…They are Scripture. They are words from God to you and me.

We must let it go. **Just forgive.** It may be hard. You may be right to be angry. They may have been completely wrong. It doesn't matter. You have been forgiven. I have been forgiven. We must forgive. No matter what and no matter how many times the person has wronged us.

Read Matthew 18:21-35. It is very clear on forgiveness. You may have read or heard it before…but it is definitely worth reading again…frequently…lest we forget.

Remember this: We are NEVER hurting the offender when we harbor unforgiveness, we are ONLY hurting ourselves!

Make allowance for each other's faults, and forgive anyone who offends you. Remember, the Lord forgave you, so you must forgive others. - Colossians 3:13

I urge you to search deep in your heart. Pray. Be sure that you have let go of all wrongs done to you. Let go of all animosity. Let go of all anger and hostility--no matter how big the wrong. No matter how wrong they were. Release it.

Unforgiveness will cost us more than we realize.

His Goodness

When we consider the Goodness of our King, it should compel us to walk in the spirit and choose the fruit of goodness for our own lives.

The Lord is good. I can think of countless situations in my life where His goodness (manifested in compassion, mercy, and forgiveness) brought me out of very dark places. You should take some time to meditate every day on the goodness He has shown to you in your life.

No time? Yes, there is: in the shower, driving here and there, as you lay in bed, or while cooking, cleaning, showering, etc. You can also get up earlier, go to bed later, and there is right now. We say, *"We don't have time."* Yes, we do. We should always find time to think about the goodness of God and **praise** His Holy Name!

The Bible has many Scriptures on the Goodness of God. I have listed a few of my favorites.

Titus 3:4-6 ...when the goodness and loving-kindness of God our Savior to man appeared, He saved us, not because of any righteousness that we had done, but because of His own pity and mercy...

Psalm 31:19 Oh, how great is Your goodness, which You have laid up for those who fear, revere, and worship You. Goodness which You have wrought for those who trust and take refuge in You before the sons of men!

Acts 14:17 Yet He did not neglect to leave some witness of Himself, for He did you good and showed you kindness and gave you rains from heaven and fruitful seasons, satisfying your hearts with nourishment and happiness.

Psalm 145:7-9 They shall pour forth like a fountain the fame of Your great and abundant goodness and shall sing aloud of Your rightness and justice. The Lord is gracious and full of compassion, slow to anger and abounding in mercy and loving-kindness. The Lord is good to all, and His tender mercies are over all His works, the entirety of His creation.

Psalm 86:5 For You, O Lord, are good, and ready to forgive our trespasses, letting them go completely and forever; and You are abundant in mercy and loving-kindness to all those who call upon You.

And let's not forget the Israelites in the Book of Exodus. They wandered around the desert for forty years... griping, complaining, unthankful, and unfaithful. Yet, our loving and merciful God still fed them every day, kept them safe, and even prevented their shoes from aging!

God is GOOD! We should never forget His goodness. If we would just reflect on His goodness in our lives and the Scriptures, we would have a whole lot more peace.

He is good!

And, because He is good: goodness in all its forms should be manifested in the lives of His children in order to be the attracting light in this lost world...

Goodness - Study Guide

Let's Pray:

Lord, thank You for all of the goodness You have shown me in my life. Thank You for your forgivensss. Help me to forgive others as You have so freely forgiven me. Please help me to see others (even people I think are hopeless, or do not think the way I think) the way you do. Help me to show Your love and compassion to all people and all situations all the time. Remind me that I too am in need of forgiveness and mercy. Help me to have eyes to see and ears to hear the needs of others. Help me to find creative ways to show kindness to people around me. Help me to let Your light shine. Help me to be a living example of Your Great Goodness. In Jesus' Mighty Name, Amen.

Memorize:

Be gentle and forbearing with one another and, if one has a difference (a grievance or complaint) against another, readily pardoning each other; even as the Lord has freely forgiven you, so you must also forgive. - Colossians 3:13

Dig Deeper:

"You have heard that it was said, 'Eye for eye, and tooth for tooth.' But I tell you, Do not resist an evil person. If someone strikes you on the right cheek, turn to him the other also. And if someone wants to sue you and take your tunic, let him have your cloak as well. If someone forces you to go one mile, go with him two miles. Give to the one who asks you, and do not turn away from the one who wants to borrow from you. - Matthew 5:38-42

Jesus is so awesome! What an incredible Person He must have been. I cannot wait to meet Him one day!

Can you imagine a society where people actually gave others a break? A place where mercy abounded? A world where we stopped judging others and allowed the King to judge hearts, and we just loved them and showed them the fruit of goodness? A society where people forgave quickly? Personally, I think it would be wonderful. Instead, we live in a society where you can get sued for millions of dollars if someone spills hot coffee from your establishment on themselves... a place where we judge others as if we have no sin in our own hearts and lives... a place where we walk around with anti this and anti that signs but have no love, mercy, or forgiveness in our hearts... a sad place... filled with sin and hatred.

I think that the point Jesus was trying to make here was this, LIGHTEN UP! Give others--and yourself a break: Stop having unrealistic expectations and needing to have justice. Be kind. Have mercy. Forgive and give more than is deserved. Love... really LOVE!

Scripture Study:

Look up the following Scriptures. I encourage you to really dig deep here and study them, look up any references and pray over them!

- Matthew 6:14-15
- Jude 1:22
- Psalm 86:11
- Mark 11:25
- Ephesians 4:31-32
- Matthew 18:21-35
- Proverbs 16:18
- Ezekiel 11:19
- Ephesians 4:26
- Hebrews 12:14-15
- Luke 6:36-37
- James 2:13

- Proverbs 16:5
- James 4:6
- Romans 12:10-17
- Philippians 2:3

Also, for an even deeper study, look up the following words in your concordance: *mercy, goodness, merciful, forgive, pride,* and study the Scripture references.

Fruit of Peace

Peace is something that I believe every human being on the plant craves in some form. There are so many ways to view peace and it means different things to different people. However, I believe that God's Word shows us the kind of peace that no one would deny obtaining, and it also teaches us how to have it!

Join me as we "bite" into the fruit of peace…

But the fruit of the Spirit is love, joy, peace, longsuffering, gentleness, goodness, faith, meekness, temperance: against such there is no law. And they that are Christ's have crucified the flesh with the affections and lusts. If we live in the Spirit, let us also walk in the Spirit. - Galatians 5:22-23

The Greek word for **peace** is – **eirene** (i-ray'-nay): *peace, quietness, rest.* The Webster's dictionary defines it as: *freedom from anxiety, annoyance, or other mental disturbances. A state of tranquility or serenity.*

Sounds great. How can I get some? Right? Well, from what I have been studying in the Word for this fruit; I have discovered that this kind of peace is a gift from God and a choice to receive. It is already ours. It has already been given. However, <u>we must choose to have this kind of peace.</u>

Jesus used the same word for peace several times in the Word. In *John 14:27 He said, Peace I leave with you; My own peace I now give and bequeath to you. Not as the world gives do I give to you. Do not let your hearts be troubled, neither let them be afraid. Stop allowing yourselves to be agitated and disturbed; and do not permit yourselves to be fearful and intimidated and cowardly and unsettled.*

I really love the Amplified Bible. However, I also want to share with you the New Living translation: *I am leaving you with a gift—*

peace of mind and heart. And the peace I give is a gift the world cannot give. So don't be troubled or afraid.

It is a GIFT. Jesus freely gave it to us. He said it right there… Peace I leave you…MY OWN peace--His peace. The world and all of its methods for obtaining peace cannot even touch the kind of peace that the King of Kings and Lord of Lords has already given you!

Now we know it is a free gift. However, we must choose. He said it right there; **Do not let**… It is our choice to let our hearts be troubled and lose our peace. We do not have to allow it. Jesus already gave us the peace. We must, by faith, believe that we already have it, and not "let" ourselves lose our peace.

A couple chapters later Jesus says in *John 16:33… in Me you may have perfect peace and confidence. In the world you have tribulation and trials and distress and frustration; but be of good cheer! For I have overcome the world. I have deprived it of power to harm you and have conquered it for you.*

YAY! All we have to do is believe what He said and receive it. You may think that it sounds almost too simple. Well, to be honest with you, most things in God's Word are. I think that is why so many of us have trouble receiving it. We are so used to the world we live in. We are used to everything having a thorough explanation, and the Word is just the opposite. God speaks simply, so that we may understand and be able to walk in victory. When the enemy comes to rob your peace, you must stand firm and know that it is yours--and he cannot take it from you without your consent.

Remember, peace is already yours. Jesus said it. God cannot lie. You can know that it is the Truth--His Truth. You must by faith believe what He says, and receive what He has already given you. The only way you are going to do that is to get the Word in you.

So that when the enemy comes knocking, you can slam the door in his slimy little face.

Yahweh Shalom

And Gideon built an altar to the Lord there and named it Yahweh-Shalom (which means "the Lord is peace"). The altar remains in Ophrah in the land of the clan of Abiezer to this day. - Judges 6:24

Yahweh Shalom means: God is Peace.

(Note: you may have heard it as Jehovah Shalom. However, Jehovah is not actually a Hebrew word. It came later. The correct word is Yahweh.)

Shalom (shaw-lome') or (shaw-lam') means: *safe, happy, health, prosperity, be safe in mind, body or estate, be at peace.*

I also looked in the thesaurus for the opposite of peace and here is what I found: *conflict, turmoil, disorder, and chaos.*

Yikes! I would much rather have the peace that God has for me!

Peace is something most people crave. We strive for it. We search for how to get it. We WANT to have peace.

What is the significance of Yahweh Shalom? And, how do we obtain this peace?

To find this out, we must dig deeper into the Word and find the hidden treasure of Shalom. The first thing that we need to understand is that <u>peace is a promise of God</u>. And, like all of God's promises, <u>we must understand the clauses</u>. We must also understand that faith plays a major role in everything that involves God.

Below are a few of our promises for peace. I strongly encourage you to read and STUDY the Scripture references.

Peace comes through Faith in Jesus Christ. (Romans 5:1)

A thankful and unselfish heart brings peace. (Philippians 4:4-7)

The Holy Spirit was the gift of peace. (John 14:26-27)

Peace is a fruit of the Spirit given as we grow in obedience. (Galatians 5:22)

Peace is an undeserved blessing from God. (Psalm 29:11)

Peace came through the shed Blood of Jesus Christ. (Colossians 1:20)

These Scriptures help us understand that peace is a free and promised gift from our Father in Heaven. Now, we must understand God's role for peace.

Yahweh Shalom

His peace is our protection. Our assurance. Our safety.

Be Merciful and gracious to me, O God, be merciful and gracious to me, for my soul takes refuge and finds shelter in You: Yes, in the shadow of Your wings will I take refuge and be confident until destructive storms have passed. Psalm 57:1

David understood that God was Yahweh Shalom. He understood that he had God's peace in him. He had faith in this. That is why he was confident living under the shadow of the Almighty God of Peace.

Finally, Yahweh Shalom, our God of Peace loves us all so very much. His desire is that ALL of His beloved children live in the peace and assurance of His unmerited favor and Grace. His peace is a gift. It is YOURS and mine for the taking.

We just need to believe what God's Word says, and be willing to walk in obedience. And, when we fail, we need to pick ourselves up, dust off, and get right back on the path God has for each of us: a path of peace. The path that Yahweh Shalom has already paved for us!

Feet Shod with Preparation of Peace

Peace is also armor!

And your feet shod with the preparation of the gospel of peace. - Ephesians 6:15

Let's look at the original Greek…

shod – hupodeo (hoop-od-eh'-o): *Put on shoes or sandals. Bind on.*

preparation – hetoimasia (het-oy-mas-ee'-ah): *Firm footing for the foundation.*

I like what **The Complete Word Study Greek Dictionary,** *by Spiros Zodhiates Th.D.* said about **preparation**… *"This intimates the firm and solid knowledge of the gospel in which the believer may stand firm and unmoved like soldiers in their military duty. The Roman soldiers were furnished with shoes that had cleats on the soles for this purpose."*

We are in a battle, friends. We are not being told to put on armor for the fun of it. **This is WAR.** We must go into battle properly prepared.

Peace that comes from the knowledge of the Word. The peace that all of us have inherited through the Precious Blood of Jesus Christ. The peace that comes from knowing that no matter what trials and tribulations we suffer here on earth, we have an eternity in all the splendor of Heaven with our Father.

There is another side of peace that I think is VERY important to being properly equipped for the battle at hand:

It is being a person who pursues peace.

A person who will seek peace to the point of giving up the need to be right.

A person who desires and maintains peace in all circumstances.

Peacemakers.

Blessed are the Peacemakers

Blessed are the peacemakers, for they will be called the children of God. - Matthew 5:9

Let's start with some word meanings…

The original Greek word for **peacemakers** in this text is eirenopoios (i-ray-nop-oy-os') and means, *pacificatory*

I looked pacificatory and related words up in the Webster's dictionary.

Pacificatory – the act of pacifying or the state of being pacified, appeased

Pacify - to bring or restore to a state of peace or tranquility…to make peace

Peace – a state of harmony between people or groups; freedom from dissension

Peace – Makers…for they will be called the children of God. There is another Scripture that says… *"you will know them by their fruit."* If we are argumentative and constantly having dissension in our lives, how can anyone consider us Christians? We will look like the dying, sinful world we live in….certainly NOT *"children of God."*

Making and maintaining peace can be a difficult thing--especially when we are "obviously right." We have this need to be right. We have this need to allow offense to rear its ugly head. We have this need to allow dissension and discord to creep into the Body.

This "need" comes from our flesh. It wars against our spirit man and always wants the opposite of what is right. We must lay our flesh down and swallow our pride. We must train ourselves to be peacemakers. Then the world will see who and Whose we really are. Then we will have a real testimony, and the credibility to bring the lost to Christ--instead of looking like hypocrites...

Blessed are the peacemakers.

When a Man's Ways...

I would like to close our study of **peace** by looking at Proverbs 16:7...

When a man's ways please the Lord, He makes even his enemies to be at peace with him. - Proverbs 16:7

At first glance, we may miss something. However, if we take a minute to think about what this verse is saying, we may be surprised!

If we live our lives for the Lord, we know through His Word that there are MANY promises we can and will receive. However, this is an amazing promise of peace...

...He makes even his enemies to be at peace with him.

It is hard enough to remain in peace with our loved ones, spouses, friends, co-workers and sisters & brothers in Christ. Yet, if our lives are lived for the Lord and our walk (because of our obedience) is pleasing to our Father in Heaven, EVEN OUR ENEMIES will be at peace with us!

I find this to be incredible!

Living in peace with ANYONE can be difficult if you are in relationship with them for a long period of time. To have the kind of peace mentioned in this Scripture would be fantastic!

However, as with all of God's promises, there is a doing on **our** part. Obedience is required. We must CHOOSE to live for Him and obey His precepts. Not only for the promises, but because of our love and appreciation for all that He is, all that He did and does for us! How could we NOT want to walk with our Lord and submit our lives to Him??

Let me leave you with one final Scripture to meditate on that, in my opinion, is the doorway to peace of mind...

Don't worry about anything; instead, pray about everything. Tell God what you need, and thank Him for all He has done. Then you will experience God's peace, which exceeds anything we can understand. His peace will guard your hearts and minds as you live in Christ Jesus. And now, dear brothers and sisters, one final thing. Fix your thoughts on what is true, and honorable, and right, and pure, and lovely, and admirable. Think about things that are excellent and worthy of praise. - Philippians 4:6-8

Peace - Study Guide

Let's Pray:

Lord, thank You for taking care of me. Thank You for supplying all of my needs. Thank You for caring about the things that matter to me. Thank You for wanting my burdens so that I don't have to carry the load. Lord, I can't carry the load any longer. Please take the burden of (fill in the blank). I just give it to You. I trust You with it. Thank You for loving me enough to take this burden from me. I choose to cast my cares on You! I choose to walk the road of peace. I choose to allow You to cultivate the fruit of peace in my heart and life. Praise Your Holy Name! In Jesus' Mighty Name, Amen.

Memorize:

Therefore humble yourselves [demote, lower yourselves in your own estimation] under the mighty hand of God, that in due time He may exalt you, Casting the whole of your care--all your anxieties, all your worries, all your concerns, once and for all on Him, for He cares for you affectionately and cares about you watchfully. - 1 Peter 5:6-7

Dig Deeper:

In the Webster's dictionary **anxious** means: *full of mental distress or uneasiness because of fear of danger or misfortune, worried.* The thesaurus had an even clearer picture: *tense, uptight, troubled, disquieted, concerned, fretful, alarmed, over-wrought, anguished, and fearful.*

This does not sound like an emotion that is pleasant to live with.

Let's look at Luke 12:22-30:

And Jesus said to His disciples, Therefore I tell you, do not be anxious and troubled with cares about your life, as to what you will have to eat; or about your body, as to what you will have to wear.

When financial troubles come, we quickly forget that our God cares for us, and wants to provide for our needs. When we worry and fret about what we will eat, how we will clothe our children, and troubling situations in our lives, we are hindering the help that He so longs to provide us with. It does not just fall in our laps. We must have faith. If Jesus says not to be anxious, then we should obey and not worry. We must trust Him.

For life is more than food, and the body more than clothes.

This is very true… our lives here are just a grain of sand in the vast Universe. There are more pressing matters…like the salvation of the lost.

Observe and consider the ravens; for they neither sow nor reap, they have neither storehouse nor barn; and yet God feeds them. Of how much more worth are you than the birds!

Have you ever seen a bird falling apart over what it will eat, or how it will find its next meal? Have you ever seen them afraid to fly? Their feathers are never in a ruffle… ever. They know the Creator has already provided. And if He has already provided for the birds… don't you think He has you covered? You are after all one of His daughters.

And which of you by being overly anxious and troubled with cares can add a cubit to his stature or a moment of time to his age [the length of his life]?

The only thing we will do by living lives with worry and anxiety is shorten our days.

If then you are not able to do such a little thing as that, why are you anxious and troubled with cares about the rest?

This verse just shows the awesome power of Almighty God. To Him, adding time to a life is a simple task. If we would just realize that He really is that powerful…why would we worry about the rest?

Consider the lilies, how they grow. They neither [wearily] toil nor spin nor weave; yet I tell you, even Solomon in all his glory (his splendor and magnificence) was not arrayed like one of these.

But if God so clothes the grass in the field, which is alive today, and tomorrow is thrown into the furnace, how much more will He clothe you, O you people of little faith?

Think about the beauty of a flower. He put such care into each kind of flower. They are all so different…yet beautiful. Shouldn't we have faith enough to know that He would clothe His own children?

And you, do not seek [by meditating and reasoning to inquire into] what you are to eat and what you are to drink; nor be of anxious (troubled) mind unsettled, excited, worried, and in suspense;

This takes it beyond mere food and clothing. When you are anxious about a pregnancy, health of a loved one, a business venture, your car starting, money to fix the car, money period, a test result, when your children are away from you, etc. (If your issue was not mentioned…it still counts! **You need not worry for nothing!**

For all the pagan world is greedily seeking these things, and your Father knows that you need them.

Your Father knows what you need. Trust Him.

When worry threatens to knock on the door of your mind pull these Scriptures out and speak them OUT LOUD over your circumstances. Those little worry demons will go running… And when they forget Whose you are and come back… pull those weapons out again and repeat!

Scripture Study:

Look up the following Scriptures. I encourage you to really dig deep here and study them, look up any references and pray over them!

- Romans 8:6
- John 14:27
- Ephesians 2:14
- Colossians 3:15
- II Timothy 2:22
- Hebrews 12:14
- James 3:18
- I Peter 3:11
- Philippians 4:6-7
- Psalm 37:11
- Philippians 4:19

Also, for an even deeper study, look up the following words in your concordance: *peace, peaceful, peacemaker, pleasing the Lord, worry, anxious,* and study the Scripture references.

Fruit of Faith

This entire fruit of the spirit series has been very eye-opening so far, and our faith study will be just as revealing…

So then faith cometh by hearing, and hearing by the Word of God.
- Romans 10:17

In order for our faith to develop and grow properly, we must "water" it with the Word. Getting the Word in us will remind us of all the reasons to trust God, and remember all of the promises that we are entitled to.

I encourage you to write down the faith Scriptures that we go over in this book, and remind yourself frequently of what God has done, is doing, and will do. Review what faith did for our brothers and sisters in the Bible. Let the Word come alive on the inside of you, and then you will acquire great faith!

But the fruit of the Spirit is love, joy, peace, longsuffering, gentleness, goodness, faith, meekness, temperance: against such there is no law. And they that are Christ's have crucified the flesh with the affections and lusts. If we live in the Spirit, let us also walk in the Spirit. - Galatians 5:22-23

In the original Greek the word **faith** is **pistis** (pis'-tis) and means; *credence, conviction of religious truth, or truthfulness of God. Reliance upon Christ for Salvation, constancy in such profession, assurance, belief, believe, fidelity.*

Why is it so hard for us to simply believe what God says? Why do we doubt? It amazes me how quickly we will embrace the lies of the devil and then doubt God--the very one Who loves us more than any person ever could.

God says... He will never leave us or forsake us. Do we believe it? No. We leave Him and then assume that He has left us. When all along He was right there holding us up, loving us, and wanting so much for us to come back to Him.

God says...We are the head and not the tail and that no weapon formed against us shall prosper. Do we believe it? No. We complain about how bad the enemy is attacking us and act like we are weak. When we should be standing firm against the attack and putting the slimy worm in his place.

God says... He loves us and wants us for His very own. Do we believe it? No. We condemn ourselves for every mistake and think that He is out to get us.

God says... He is the Great Physician. Do we believe it? No. When we get sick we accept it as part of life and allow the sickness to wreak havoc on our bodies--when the Word says that by His stripes we are healed. Jesus didn't accept those whips for the fun of it. He was suffering so that we may be well. The problem is that we don't believe it, and receive it, and proclaim it. We accept the illness instead of the healing for it.

God says a lot of things. There are countless promises in the Word that we either overlook or simply don't accept. We must believe to receive. The Word says that without faith it is impossible to please God. We must believe that He is to even be saved. We must study the Word and learn all the gifts and promises that He desires to give us. We will never receive them if we do not believe.

Let's explore further, though, just WHAT faith is...

What is it and How does it Work?

Hebrews 11 has a lot to say about faith. Let's begin with the Biblical definition of faith:

Now faith is the substance of things hoped for, the evidence of things not seen. Hebrews 11:1

First, I want to look at **substance** and **evidence** in their original Greek.

Substance – hupostasis (hoop-os'-tas-is): assurance guarantee, reality, essence, confidence, that which is the basis of something.

Evidence – elegchos (el'-eng-khos): proof, conviction, persuasion.

The Amplified Bible puts it nicely…

Now faith is the assurance (the confirmation, the title deed) of the things we hope for, being the proof of things we do not see and the conviction of their reality [faith perceiving as real fact what is not revealed to the senses].

And of course, the Webster's dictionary definition…

Faith – confidence or trust in a person or thing.

We must have faith to even be a Christian. You must believe that Jesus really is the Son of God, died on the cross for your sins, and rose on the third day. We were not there. We did not actually "see" all of this occur. However, we believe it. Why? Because we have FAITH in what the Word says. We have FAITH that our sins are forgiven, and that Jesus is sitting at the Right Hand of the Father speaking on our behalf.

That is what faith is--believing without seeing.

Through faith we understand that the worlds were framed by the Word of God, so that things which are seen were not made of things which do appear. Hebrews 11:3

This is another example of faith that we already have. We must believe that God created the universe with His Words. We were not there...we did not see it....**we believe without seeing**. We have faith.

How many of us have said, "I wish I had faith like so and so..." we do! We just need to learn how to develop and exercise our faith. It's like working out. If you don't exercise you will not be in "good shape." On the other hand, when you exercise regularly, you feel better and you look better.

I want you to think about all of the faith that you already have. We mentioned two so far: your Salvation and the Creation. Now, I want to encourage you to take some time to think of how you are already exercising your faith. Once you begin to realize it is already there, it will be easier for you to see how faith works...

Faith Makes things Happen

By faith Abel offered unto God a more excellent sacrifice than Cain, by which he obtained witness that he was righteous, God testifying of his gifts... - Hebrews 11:4a

I would like to start by looking at two words in their original Greek meanings...

Excellent - **pleion** (pli'-on): figuratively of worth, importance, dignity, meaning more, greater, higher, to abound.

Testifying - **martureo** (mar-too-reh'-o): emphatically, to testify strongly, bear honorable testimony, to be well testified about, to have good witness.

It wasn't so much "what" they gave that made one better than the other. It was "how" they gave. Abel gave the first born of his sheep. That was a HUGE step of faith. Cain gave with the wrong heart and motive. He gave without faith. God was more pleased with Abel's offering because of the FAITH behind it. He even went so far as to testify about it.

Can you imagine God, Himself, speaking well about you? Can you imagine the King of Kings bearing good witness about your offering? Well, you don't have to imagine, **if** you give by faith, with a pure heart and motive.

We can give and give and give without ever pleasing God. Giving in and of itself is fine. However, when we give by **faith**, we are going to a whole new level. Please don't misunderstand me, you cannot just give to get. It's not only a matter of faith, it is a matter of the **heart**. Faith is what will sow the seed properly. The right heart is what will help it to reap a good harvest.

I encourage you to pray about how you can give a "faith offering." Do not limit yourself to *materialistic* things. You can offer your time or talents too. The point of the exercise is to help you to **develop** your faith. If you never use your faith, it will never become all that God intended it to be.

Keep this in mind…Not one person was healed by Jesus while He was here, that did not already BELIEVE that He could heal them. **Faith is what makes things happen!**

I hope that all of this is making sense to you…

Faith at Work

Hebrews 11:7-16: Prompted by faith Noah, being forewarned by God concerning events of which as yet there was no visible sign, took heed and diligently and reverently constructed and prepared an ark for the deliverance of his own family. By this, his faith which relied on God, he passed judgment and sentence on the world's unbelief and became an heir and possessor of righteousness (that relation of being right into which God puts the person who has faith).

Can you imagine being the ONLY family building this ark? This was **major** faith at work.

Urged on by faith Abraham, when he was called, obeyed and went forth to a place which he was destined to receive as an inheritance; and he went, although he did not know or trouble his mind about where he was to go.

Abraham had no idea where he was going. However, he <u>chose</u> to believe God.

Prompted by faith he dwelt as a temporary resident in the land which was designated in the promise of God, though he was like a stranger in a strange country, living in tents with Isaac and Jacob, fellow heirs with him of the same promise.

For he was waiting expectantly and confidently, looking forward to the city which has fixed and firm foundations, whose Architect and Builder is God.

He NEVER gave up. He did not allow his faith to waver!

Because of faith also Sarah herself received physical power to conceive a child, even when she was long past the age for it, because she considered God, Who had given her the promise to be reliable and trustworthy and true to His word.

So from one man, though he was physically as good as dead, there have sprung descendants whose number is as the stars of heaven and as countless as the innumerable sands on the seashore.

Can you imagine the faith it took for an old woman to give birth? Sarah exercised her faith while she carried and delivered Isaac.

These people came to the end of their days controlled and sustained by their faith, even though many of them never received the tangible fulfillment of God's promises. They only saw it, by faith, in the distance. All the while acknowledging and confessing that they were strangers, temporary residents, and exiles upon the earth.

They did not need to ever "see" the promises with their natural eyes. They walked in the spirit and had faith. They took God at His Word. They knew and understood that God does what He says He will do!

Now those people who talk as they did show plainly that they are in search of a fatherland (their own country).

If they had been thinking with [homesick] remembrance of that country from which they were emigrants, they would have found constant opportunity to return to it.

But the truth is that they were yearning for and aspiring to a better and more desirable country, that is, a heavenly [one]. For that reason God is not ashamed to be called their God [even to be surnamed their God--the God of Abraham, Isaac, and Jacob], for He has prepared a city for them.

They are true examples of aliens. They understood that they were not of this world. By faith they saw a better place that God had for them. They looked on by faith to their true home. They did not need to "see" it, they **believed** God!

We can ALL learn a lot about faith and how to trust in God's Word. There are <u>many</u> examples from those who lived before us. We can see how they exercised their faith, and how they never wavered in their faith.

We cannot allow our senses to rule us. We must live our lives by faith. We must **believe** what God says. When we get this into our thick skulls, we will finally be getting somewhere in our walk. We will no longer be weak and fragile; instead we will be strong and fight for the Kingdom by FAITH!

Faith Comes by Hearing

*So then faith cometh by hearing, and hearing by the word of God. -
Romans 10:17*

I had such a revelation when I dug deeper into what this verse is really saying. I have read it many times. Let me share the treasure I uncovered…

I looked up all of the words in their original Greek and they are all basically cut and dry. They mean what they say. So, I asked the Lord, "OK, what am I supposed to find?" I heard, "Get your Thesaurus." I did. I looked up each word and discovered something very interesting about the words, "come" and "hearing" in their antonym (opposite) forms.

I always like to look at the "flip side" as I call it. What does it mean if I do not do this… or if I turn the word around? Many times it opens a whole new world for me.

Let's take a look.

Come – go, go away, depart, leave, withdraw, and retreat.

Hearing – ignore, reject, disapprove, and disagree with.

You see, when we are not listening to what the word says, a.k.a. GOD, we are telling faith to leave, depart, and go away. We are ignoring, rejecting, and disagreeing with God.

What we *hear* **matters**--whether it is coming from a music player, movie, television, or people in our lives. What we HEAR directly affects what will come. Faith COMES by HEARING.

Romans 10:17 is telling us the source of where faith comes from. It comes from HEARING the Word of God.

Let me give you some practical examples:

We will not find the faith we need to help a dying marriage if what we are hearing is all about infidelity, casual sex, and sinful programming. However, we CAN find the faith to go on; if we study God's Word and **speak** it out so we **hear** it. We could also get the faith we need to save our marriage, when we listen to a good Christian marriage teaching series.

We will not find our way to the purpose that God has for us if we listen to what people say. If we listen to others criticize, belittle, or try to change what we know God has called us to do, we will fail. We will begin to doubt and question what we know. However, if we are careful about **who** we let speak into our lives, we will save ourselves a heap of trouble.

If we are teaching our children purity, and let them listen to sexually explicit lyrics; we are harming them and setting them up to fail. They will **believe** what they **hear**. Do not think for a minute that just because you are saying it, you can counteract the lyrics that they listen to over and over again. We need to teach them to guard their ears.

We will not have the strength to live a consecrated life in this dark world if we allow an overload of the culture into our head. If all we listen to is the world's news… the world's music… the world's entertainment… the world's causes… the world's belief system…We will begin to have a worldly mentality. We will begin to find ways to adapt God's Word to the culture. We will begin to find ways to make *excuses* for what we KNOW is sin. **We will lose the good fight!**

Fight the good fight of the faith; lay hold of the eternal life to which you were summoned, and for which you confessed the good confession of faith before many witnesses. - I Timothy 6:12

How can we fight the good fight of faith if we are telling faith to leave, depart, and go away? How can we fight the good fight of faith if we are ignoring, rejecting, and disagreeing with God by not hearing the Word of God?

Think about this…

The flip side of faith is: *doubt, uncertainty, skepticism, unbelief, mistrust, denial, dissent, discredit, infidelity, rejection, agnosticism.*

Beware of what you allow yourself to hear.

So then faith cometh by hearing, and hearing by the word of God. - Romans 10:17

Final Thoughts on Faith

Even so faith, if it hath not works, is dead, being alone. - James 2:17

There must be <u>action</u> behind the faith. We must have a personal relationship with Jesus Christ. The kind of faith mentioned in the Word is not for the world. It is for the children of God. It is a **gift** He gives us. What else can you call something that "moves mountains"? Put your faith into ACTION!

For we walk by faith, not by sight. - 2 Corinthians 5:7

Faith has nothing to do with our senses. We cannot rely on our eyes. They will **always** lie. We must believe through the eyes of our faith. If we use our fleshly eyes we will **never** see anything other than the impossible. However, with God, <u>ALL things are possible</u>!

FAITH is what moves God. Faith is what pleases God.

The next time you are exercising (believing) your faith, and you don't "see" anything happening, remember this: **Faith is believing without seeing!** Faith is <u>trusting</u> God and <u>believing</u> what He says. Faith is what makes you His child! Without it, you could NEVER believe that Jesus died on the cross for your sins, rose from the dead, and now sits at the Right Hand of the Father!

WALK BY FAITH NOT BY SIGHT!!!

Faith - Study Guide

Let's Pray:

Lord, thank You for loving me. Thank You for giving me Your Living Word as a blueprint on how to live my life. Help me to walk in faith. Help me to exercise my faith and believe the unseen. Help me to develop the fruit of faith, so that I may be a living witness to everyone I influence and come into contact with. I want them to KNOW and understand Your ways through the life of faith I live before them. Give me the strength and courage to do so. You are a Mighty God. You are a Loving God. You are Worthy of ALL the glory, honor, and praise. You are the First and the Last. You are the Beginning and the End. You are the great I Am. You are Merciful and Kind. I am honored and humbled by Your love for me. Thank You, my precious Daddy for loving and caring for me. Thank You. Bless the Name of my God, Who Reigns FOREVER! Holy is the Lord God Almighty. Praise You! In Jesus' Mighty Name, Amen.

Memorize:

And it is impossible to please God without faith. Anyone who wants to come to him must believe that God exists and that he rewards those who sincerely seek him. - Hebrews 11:6

Dig Deeper:

Let's look at how faith was put in action by those who came before us...

Hebrews 11:17-29 (KJV)

By faith Abraham, when he was tried, offered up Isaac: and he that had received the promises offered up his only begotten son,

Of whom it was said, That in Isaac shall thy seed be called:

Accounting that God was able to raise him up, even from the dead; from whence also he received him in a figure.

Abraham loved and trusted God more than anything. He knew that God would NEVER go back on His Word. So, He was willing to sacrifice Isaac, because he knew that God would make a way to keep His promise. He was a GREAT man of faith. How many of us would be willing to exercise that kind of faith?

By faith Isaac blessed Jacob and Esau concerning things to come.

By faith Jacob, when he was a dying, blessed both the sons of Joseph; and worshipped, leaning upon the top of his staff.

By faith Joseph, when he died, made mention of the departing of the children of Israel; and gave commandment concerning his bones.

These men looked to the future by faith. They knew that better days were coming. They didn't have to "see," they simply had faith.

By faith Moses, when he was born, was hid three months of his parents, because they saw he was a proper child; and they were not afraid of the king's commandment.

By faith Moses, when he was come to years, refused to be called the son of Pharaoh's daughter;

Choosing rather to suffer affliction with the people of God, than to enjoy the pleasures of sin for a season;

Esteeming the reproach of Christ greater riches than the treasures in Egypt: for he had respect unto the recompense of the reward.

By faith he forsook Egypt, not fearing the wrath of the king: for he endured, as seeing him who is invisible.

Through faith he kept the Passover, and the sprinkling of blood, lest he that destroyed the firstborn should touch them.

By faith they passed through the Red sea as by dry land: which the Egyptians assaying to do were drowned.

Moses was a wonderful example of faith at work. He left the comforts of the palace to fulfill the call of God. He dealt with an ungodly king and a bunch of complainers. He was treasured by God because he BELIEVED God. He put down his staff and parted the red sea by faith. He believed what God had told him. He lived by faith!

I want to encourage you to trust in the One Who created all things. Any one of us can have the kind of faith that moves mountains. It is already living on the inside of us. We just need to believe and exercise it.

One final thing I want to point out.

Faith is the opposite of fear. So, if you lack faith, fear is the culprit. Whom or what have you to fear with God on your side??

If God is for us, who can be against us? [Who can be our foe, if God is on our side?] - Romans 8:31b

Scripture Study:

Look up the following Scriptures. I encourage you to really dig deep here and study them, look up any references and pray over them!

- Hebrews 13:6

- Ephesians 2:8

- 2 Corinthians 5:7

- Psalm 23:4

- Mark 9:23

- Philippians 4:13

- Luke 17:6

- Proverbs 3:5-8
- Hebrews 11 (whole chapter)
- Ephesians 2:8-9
- 1 John 5:14
- James 1:3
- Mark 11:23
- 2 Timothy 1:7

Also, for an even deeper study, look up the following words in your concordance: *faith, doubt, believe, fear, fear not, believing God,* and study the Scripture references.

Fruit of Gentleness

Gentleness is something I have never been known for. I am a bit assertive and can be someone's iron in the old "iron sharpens iron" Scripture. In its place has been anger brought on by years of abuse and pain. Anger is the easiest emotion to tap into, and why many of us never reach our full potential in Christ.

God designed us to be balanced. Anger in and of itself is not sin. However, when we sin in our anger, we are out of alignment.

The fruit of Gentleness is what brings about balance to anger...

But the fruit of the Spirit is love, joy, peace, longsuffering, gentleness, goodness, faith, meekness, temperance: against such there is no law. And they that are Christ's have crucified the flesh with the affections and lusts. If we live in the Spirit, let us also walk in the Spirit. - Galatians 5:22-23

If you struggle with anger at all you may find this topic very interesting.

We will start with the Greek text.

Gentleness - **chrestos** (khrase-tos') or **chrestotes** (khray-stot'-ace): gracious, kind, excellence in character or demeanor, goodness, kindness.

What does gracious and kind mean? You may know, but let's look anyway.

Gracious - Pleasantly kind, benevolent, courteous, merciful, compassionate.

Kind - Considerate or helpful. Mild and gentle.

Life can get pretty frustrating for anyone--even if you are a Christian. Look at the following questions and see if any of them are true in your life...

- Have you ever yelled at your children, a friend or even a stranger?

- Have you ever experienced a bit of road rage? Maybe flicked off another driver?

- Have you ever been sarcastic with your spouse?

- Have you ever been rude? Ever?

- Have you ever felt unsympathetic towards a homeless person to the point where you thought angrily, "Get a job"?

- Seriously, have you ever lost your temper... even just a little??

These are just a few. The point is: we can all benefit from more kindness in our attitudes and demeanor.

There are no quick fixes or concrete answers on how to accomplish being a better version of ourselves--other than getting the Word into you and *choosing* to be kind. It will take a whole lot of effort on your part. You will feel like your going uphill most of the time. However, as with all things that God asks us to do, there are rewards...

We will be healthier. We will have lasting relationships. We will have more peace. We will stay in relationship with our children when they grow up. We will have a happier marriage. We will feel happier. And most importantly, we will please our Savior.

A little kindness goes a long way, my dear readers. The more you give it the more you will receive it. That is another benefit to kindness. Think about the spiritual law of sowing and reaping. What you put in comes out and what you put out will come back to you.

Anger Hinders Gentleness

Cease from anger and forsake wrath; fret not yourself–it tends only to evildoing. - Psalm 37:8

Anger.

After many years of struggle with it, I was able to pinpoint its origin in my life a few years back. I took a course that basically does a spiritual "deep cleaning." I discovered it came from my childhood. I was not only raised in an angry environment, I had a mother who was consumed with anger and bitterness. Another thing that helped anger develop in my heart was the years of sexual abuse that I endured as a young child. Anyone who has been sexually abused has anger. Yes, I believe this with all of my heart. Why? Because someone stole something from them, hurt them deeply, and they were too small and weak to stop it. THAT can make you angry.

Most of my anger is left over from the sexual abuse. My heart struggles with it so deeply. I say things like: "NO one is going to hurt me like that again"…"I will not let anyone penetrate my force field of protection"…etc.

I am a very strong woman. I am happy to be strong, discerning and no nonsense. I am a fighter. Those are not bad things. However, I can also fly off the handle, become cold to others, harsh, too frank and quite abrupt. All of these traits are NOT good. Anger creeps at my door and only leads me to sin in it.

A fool vents all his feelings, But a wise man holds them back. - Proverbs 29:11

I love how God's Word is like a two edged sword and pierces my heart with His loving conviction.

I do not want to be a fool. I want to develop temperance, love, patience and mercy in my heart more and more every day. For as I do, I overcome the anger within me. How can you be angry when you are loving, showing mercy, and being patient with someone? It makes it *much* harder.

If you struggle with anger, there is hope in God's Word. His love letter to us offers many encouraging statements that are there to help us overcome our weakness. If anger is yours, bring it before His throne; ask Him to help you find the source. Once you find the source, it puts it all in perspective. It makes it easier to understand and pinpoint the triggers. Then, seek guidance from His Word. Find Scriptures on anger and learn them inside and out. Speak them. Ask Him to help you abide in Him and let go of anger. He WILL help you! He helps me every day!

Wrath and Strife...

Now the works of the flesh are manifest, which are these; Adultery, fornication, uncleanness, lasciviousness, Idolatry, witchcraft, hatred, variance, emulations, wrath, strife, seditions, heresies, envyings, murders, drunkenness, revellings, and such like: of the which I tell you before, as I have also told you in time past, that they which do such things shall not inherit the Kingdom of God. - Galatians 5:19-21

Let's take a look at some of the original Greek text:

Wrath – **thumos** (thoo-mos'): fierceness.

Strife – **erethizo** (er-eth-id'-zo) or **eritheia** (er-ith-i'-ah): to stimulate to anger, provoke, contention.

The dictionary meaning for fierceness is vehement hostility and unrestrained violence--a brutally harsh bully.

It may seem that a good Christian couldn't possibly manifest these behaviors. That assumption would be wrong--very wrong. Just because you are a Christian doesn't mean you don't have issues with sin. However, you should always be in a growing process. You should actively be seeking guidance and pastoral counseling, as well as diving into the Word and seeking the face of God.

That being said, there are many Christians that have violent tempers. You may be one. Maybe you like to slam doors and things around when you are angry. You may be a parent who is too harsh with your children and instead of spanking them in love you beat them in anger. You may be someone who is violent, loud and aggressive.

No matter how mild or extreme your violent anger is, it is wrong. You are sinning. Anger itself is not sin. What turns anger into sin is when we yell, swear, become rude, or get violent in any way.

If you know that you are someone who leans more on the extreme side, and you are afraid you may hurt others, you MUST get help immediately. God loves you and wants to heal you from the inside out. He is not angry with you. He wants you to repent and seek help. I suggest Christian counseling. The world deals with problems without God. Christian counselors are not only going to help you in a medical way, but help heal you spiritually too.

Sinful anger is an extremely destructive force. No matter how mild you "think" your anger problem might be, it is destructive.

Final Thoughts on Anger...

Understand this, my beloved brethren. Let every man be quick to hear, slow to speak, slow to take offense and get angry. For man's anger does not promote the righteousness God wishes and requires. - James 1:19-20

Anger means: a strong feeling of displeasure aroused by a real or supposed wrong, wrath.

The opposite of anger is: love, peacefulness, acceptance, forgiveness.

As, I mentioned earlier, I have been dealing with anger my whole life. God has been dealing with me about this for years. I have struggled with trying to be a "good, quiet Christian woman".

I find verse 19 to be a challenge at times. I am not always quick to hear and I can whip a slew of words out faster than a thought can form. I do not get offended too often. However, I am often the *offender*, and must ask God's forgiveness on a semi regular basis for my temper, and how quick I respond before thinking. I am much better than I used to be-- thank God. I am still a work in progress, though, and have by no means "arrived."

The best advice I can give those of you who struggle in these areas is to keep pressing in. Keep getting into the Word. Keep asking God to help you. And one day you will wake up and realize how far you have come. It will happen if you choose to never give up and never let your mistakes get you down.

That is the key. The devil loves to make us feel like dirt. He loves to throw our faults and mistakes in our faces. In order to find victory you must begin to recognize these attacks and throw it back. Stand up against the little worm. He has no authority over you. He is under your feet. Jesus put him there. The only way he can get out from under you is if you let him.

Verse 20 is what keeps me from staying down when I slip. I do not want to be the kind of person that makes my Beloved Savior look bad. I do not want to be a poor example before my children. I want my light to shine so bright that every demon in hell will be blinded, and people will know Who and what I stand for. That is why I write: to encourage and equip other Believers. To help us become all that God created us to be.

The Point: When you mess up don't give up. Get up. Brush yourself off, and move on.

Do not be quick in spirit to be angry or vexed, for anger and vexation lodge in the bosom of fools. - Ecclesiastes 7:9

Because of Your Love...

Always be humble and gentle. Be patient with each other, making allowance for each other's faults because of your love. - Ephesians 4:2

I would say that I fail miserably on a daily basis with this one. By all means, please stop reading if you have mastered Ephesians 4:2.

For those of you who struggle with being humble, gentle and patient, let's dig deeper…

To be humble is to be: submissive, meek, unassuming, polite, not proud or arrogant, and modest.

To be gentle is to be: clement, peaceful, soothing, tender, lenient, merciful, mild, temperate, tame, quiet, and courteous.

To be patient is to be: uncomplaining, long-suffering, forbearing, calm, unruffled, unexcited, composed and untiring. Patience is also able to: bear provocation, annoyance, misfortune, delay, hardship, pain, etc., with fortitude and calm and without complaint, anger, or the like.

Nope, not me!

I get aggravated, loud, impatient, tired and angry with people. I do not always make allowances for the faults of others, and people can really tick me off! I find this Scripture very challenging. However, then I think about how God looks past my faults *and loves me no matter what*. How can I deny someone the same courtesy?

How can we possibly deal with the ridiculous people we encounter each day? Better yet, how do we deal with those who are closest to us? They seem to be the ones who really push our buttons! The answer is in the Scripture as well…

...Because of your love...

Yes, Christ's love and strength is IN us, and if we choose to love, we CAN. We may need to try a bit harder dealing with some; however, we really can be gentle, kind, patient and humble with all people. We just need to realize it cannot be done through our own strength. We need to rely on the Lord to give us the strength!

Keep on asking and it will be given you; keep on seeking and you will find; keep on knocking and the door will be opened to you. - Matthew 7:7

We need to ask, seek and knock for what we need. I know that I know that I KNOW that my Daddy God is ALWAYS available and willing to assist me when I need it. It is the same for you. When we encounter difficult people or have to deal with someone on a regular basis that really annoys us, we need to refer to God's Word. We need to seek HIS help. We need to find our strength in Him.

And, **never** give up!

And as for you, brethren, do not become weary or lose heart in doing right, but continue in well-doing without weakening. - 2 Thessalonians 3:13

This is the key: we cannot allow ourselves to grow weary in well doing. We cannot lose heart. God wants to develop patience, gentleness and humility in all of us; because He loves us and knows it is the only way to true peace, joy and happiness. How can we find peace, joy and happiness, if we are living without patience and in offense, anger, annoyances and pride?

We cannot.

Only love can help us reach our goal.

Only our love for God and willingness to obey Him will ever get us on the road. Once there, the only way to walk the road of peace, joy, and happiness is through forgiveness, humility, gentleness, patience, and Christ's love in us pouring out towards others--especially difficult "others".

Gentleness - Study Guide

Let's Pray:

Lord, help me to cultivate gentleness in my life. Help me to let go of anger and learn to forgive others when I am wronged. Help me to show mercy and not judge. Teach me to love like YOU love. Convict me when I am acting in a manner that displeases You. I want to live a life that shines for You and shows the world Your loving kindness, mercy and compassion. I do not want to misrepresent you by acting out in my flesh and letting offense and unforgiveness rule me. I love You Lord. You are Worthy of all glory, honor and praise. You are an awesome God. Mighty and filled with compassion. Thank You for loving me. In Jesus' Mighty Name, Amen.

Memorize:

Be self-controlled and alert. Your enemy the devil prowls around like a roaring lion looking for someone to devour. - 1Peter 5:8

Dig Deeper:

Anger is a debilitating character flaw that can adversely affect our spiritual lives in ways we may not realize. We must learn to overcome anger, forgive, and let go of offenses. The fruit of gentleness can only be grown if anger is put in its place, and anger is really tied into unforgiveness...

Good sense makes a man restrain his anger, and it is his glory to overlook a transgression or an offense. - Proverbs 19:11

Let's break this Scripture down and dig into the meat of God's Word...

"Good sense makes a man restrain his anger,"

In the original Hebrew, **good sense**, actually comes from **sekel** and means, *wisdom*. So when we restrain our anger we are manifesting wisdom in our lives.

Let's look closely into what exactly **overlook** and **restrain** mean…

I looked them both up in the dictionary and found the following:

Overlook is to fail to notice or consider. To excuse or pardon.

In the thesaurus I found; *ignore, disregard, excuse, forgive and shrug off.*

Restrain is to hold back from action. To limit or hamper the activity, growth or effect of — to bind back.

In the thesaurus I found; *keep under control, gag, muzzle, prevent, stop, shackle, and handicap.*

This is very enlightening to me. Think about all that we have done. Think about the sin that we all commit every day. Yet, our loving and merciful God puts mercy into practice every day. He chooses to see the Blood of Jesus and chooses to pardon our mistakes. We serve a Holy God and I am certain that this world offends His holiness every moment of every day… yet… He holds back His anger on mankind.

What exactly is offense?

An offense is a violation or breaking of social or moral rule; transgression; sin. It is something that offends or displeases.

When I looked up offense in the thesaurus I found words like: *insult, disrespect, rudeness, harm, abuse, embarrass, and humiliate.*

I find this profound. Think about how many people in your life have insulted you, been rude to you, abused and humiliated you. Seriously, if we thought about it, we would find that someone does something just about every day that displeases us and opens the door for offense to be taken, and bitterness to plant itself in our hearts.

Now, flip it around and think about how you and I fail EVERY day in some area or another. We sin EVERY day. We need to repent for something EVERY day.

What does God choose to do?

He sent His Beloved Son to take our place and suffer for all of our decay so that He can look BEYOND our transgressions.

Who do we think we are to judge another man for His sin when WE sin? Who are we to hold onto an offense when we have been pardoned?

Let's see just how serious God is on the subject of offense and mercy...

For just as you judge and criticize and condemn others, you will be judged and criticized and condemned, and in accordance with the measure you use to deal out to others, it will be dealt out again to you. - Matthew 7:2.

But wait, Jesus goes even further in Matthew 18:23-35:

Therefore the kingdom of heaven is like a human king who wished to settle accounts with his attendants.

When he began the accounting, one was brought to him who owed him 10,000 talents [about $10,000,000],

And because he could not pay, his master ordered him to be sold, with his wife and his children and everything that he possessed, and payment to be made.

So the attendant fell on his knees, begging him, Have patience with me and I will pay you everything.

And his master's heart was moved with compassion, and he released him and forgave him canceling the debt.

But that same attendant, as he went out, found one of his fellow attendants who owed him a hundred denarii [about twenty dollars]; and he caught him by the throat and said, Pay what you owe!

So his fellow attendant fell down and begged him earnestly, give me time, and I will pay you all!

But he was unwilling, and he went out and had him put in prison till he should pay the debt.

When his fellow attendants saw what had happened, they were greatly distressed, and they went and told everything that had taken place to their master.

Then his master called him and said to him, you contemptible and wicked attendant! I forgave and cancelled all that great debt of yours because you begged me to.

And should you not have had pity and mercy on your fellow attendant, as I had pity and mercy on you?

And in wrath his master turned him over to the torturers (the jailers), till he should pay all that he owed.

So also My heavenly Father will deal with every one of you if you do not freely forgive your brother from your heart his offenses.

If that didn't convict you, this will...

There will be no mercy for those who have not shown mercy to others. But if you have been merciful, God will be merciful when he judges you. – James 2:13

WOW!

In closing, let's finish by looking at the last section of Proverbs 19:11…

"and it is his glory to overlook a transgression or an offense."

Hmmm… I think above three references explain this one. It is for OUR benefit to overlook an offense, and it one of the only ways to let go of anger and help with the development of the fruit of gentleness.

Let's be careful what we allow ourselves to hold onto. Let's make sure we are always prayerfully considering all angles, forgiving, showing abundant mercy, and allowing God to speak to us and use His Word as our compass.

Scripture Study:

Look up the following Scriptures. I encourage you to really dig deep here and study them, look up any references and pray over them!

- Proverbs 19:11
- Romans 12:19
- Ephesians 4:26-27
- Psalm 37:8
- Micah 6:8
- 2 Timothy 2:24-26
- Matthew 18 (whole chapter)
- Ephesians 4:2

- Matthew 6:14-15; 7:2
- James 1:19-20
- Luke 6:32 & 37
- Romans 2:1
- Colossians 3:13
- James 2:13
- 1 John 4:20
- Proverbs 14:29
- Titus 3:2
- Matthew 7:2
- James 1:19-20

Also, for an even deeper study, look up the following words in your concordance: *anger, wrath, gentle, offense, kind, gentleness, forgiveness, forgive,* and study the Scripture references.

Fruit of Love

I saved love for last, because I believe it is not only the most important fruit, it also ties all the other fruits together. You cannot have self control, meekness, longsuffering (patience), joy, goodness, peace, faith, and gentleness, if love is not involved.

Love is the main vein of the tree. It is the only thing that can help us walk in the spirit and become all that God created us to be.

Love is what helped Jesus choose to die on the cross, so that we might be free from sin and death.

Love is why we are here.

Love is everything…

But the fruit of the Spirit is love, joy, peace, longsuffering, gentleness, goodness, faith, meekness, temperance: against such there is no law. And they that are Christ's have crucified the flesh with the affections and lusts. If we live in the Spirit, let us also walk in the Spirit. - Galatians 5:22-23

The original Greek word for **love** in this text is **agape** (ag-ah'-pay): *love, affection, a love feast, dear love.*

I believe that if we take the time to really know God in a personal way through studying His Word, and having an active prayer life, we can cultivate this kind of love in our lives.

I believe that when we have truly submitted our wills to God, and allow ourselves to be rooted and grounded in love; all of the manifestations of the flesh begin to diminish. When we really get this "love" thing and live it out, then all of the other fruits are naturally there. For if we have love, we lack nothing.

When we get to a place where Jesus is truly Lord over our thoughts, actions, and lives--we start shedding our fleshly behaviors and desires. We begin to have a mind like Christ. We begin to want what He wants. We begin to grow more fruit than weeds.

The only way to get to that place is to actively pursue God. If all we do is show up for church once or twice a week, and do our nursery duty, say our little amens here and there, we are useless, and poor examples for the One Who died for our sins.

We must <u>choose</u> to have an actual *relationship* with God. Now, I don't believe in set formulas. Everyone is different and everyone has a different schedule and lifestyle. However, we should all spend time with God every day. It does not matter if it is five minutes or five hours. The point is that we desire a relationship with Him and are pursuing it the best we can.

What is Love?

I'm sure you've heard it and/or read it...

I Corinthians 13:4-8 - Love endures long and is patient and kind; love is never envious nor boils over with jealousy, it is not boastful and does not display itself haughtily. It is not conceited; it is not rude and does not act unbecomingly. Love does not insist on its own rights or its own way, for it is not self-seeking; it is not touchy or fretful or resentful; it takes no account of the evil done to it [it pays no attention to a suffered wrong]. It does not rejoice at injustice and unrighteousness, but rejoices when right and truth prevail. Love bears up under anything and everything that comes, is ever ready to believe the best of every person, its hopes are fadeless under all circumstances, and it endures everything without weakening. Love never fails...

There really isn't anything more I can add. God has explained "what" love is thoroughly.

Obviously, we don't just snap our fingers and suddenly have the kind of love described in I Corinthians. It comes gradually over time as we study and learn His Word (His ways). The Word says that **God is Love** in I John 4:16. So, if we pour enough of God into our lives and spirits, we will automatically love more like He loves. It is what naturally happens as we submit our lives to Him and His will. We grow the "fruit" of love.

We cannot beat ourselves up when we fail. The enemy would love that. We must press on. Make it a point to read I Corinthians 13 as often as you can. Get it in you, pray and learn to love God--the source of all love.

The next question would be... How?

How Do We Love Him?

Love is mentioned well over 350 times in the Bible. I'm sure God must be trying to tell us something.

Matthew 22:37-38 - And He replied to him, you shall love the Lord your God with all your heart and with all your soul and with all your mind. This is the most important and first commandment.

I am sure that we have all heard this verse many times. But, do we really get it? How do we love God? Why should we love God? Let's explore How to love God...

How Do We Love Him?

It is very simply stated by Jesus in John 14:15, *if you really love me, you will keep (obey) my commands.* As simple as it sounds… it seems to be a very difficult task… or is it? Well, yes and no. If we study the Word, get it into our hearts and minds; it is easier to submit to the Holy Spirit…

However, when we fill our minds with the world, i.e.:

Soap operas, worldly sitcoms, music, movies, books, etc. - which encourage adultery, lust, impurity, sexual innuendos, crude language, fornication, lies, deceit, provocative lyrics, and many other sinful desires …

Entertainment magazines, columns, blogs, etc. - which are filled with gossip, wrong information, slander, hurtful situations in human lives, and really none of our business anyway…

Basically, our minds become so absorbed with this unrealistic, ungodly, and sin-filled world that we lose sight of our purpose. We become desensitized to the muck. We forget our first Love and we no longer desire to spend time with our Lord. Worldly entertainment becomes our focus and the belief system of this world becomes more and more appealing. Eventually, we begin to make excuses, allowances for sin, and try to make God's Word fit the current culture.

Don't get me wrong. I am not saying that every non-Christian song, movie, or entertainment venue is sinful. I am saying be careful what goes in. It will come out in one form or another: perhaps a sinful stronghold, addiction, fear, lack of self control, worldly mindset, loss of peace, etc., etc., etc…

The Bible says in Galatians 6:7 that we reap what we sow. If we sow junk into our minds we will reap junk. For example, if you are searching radio looking for a good song to listen to… make sure it is good for your spirit, not your flesh.

You may be thinking I have gone too far, or that I don't know what I'm talking about. Yes, I do. I know because the Word tells me so.

In I John 2:15 it says, do not love or cherish the world or the things that are in the world. If anyone loves the world, love for the Father is not in him. For all that is in the world – the lust of the flesh and the lust of the eyes and the pride of life or stability of earthly things – these do not come from the Father, but are from the world itself. And the world passes away and disappears, and with it the forbidden cravings of it; but he who does the will of God and carries out His purposes in his life abides forever.

Think about it this way:

Would you only feed your body once or twice a week? No, of course not! We stuff our faces every day! Don't you think our spirits should be fed daily as well? And, not junk food. Our spirits need nutritious food just like our bodies in order to be healthy, strong, and able to overcome the sin and lusts of this godless world. We must begin to rise up, and take a stand in our own lives, if we ever hope to make a difference in this lost world!

Letting go of this world is the first step in how we love Him.

Why Should We Love Him?

I'm sure this would seem like an obvious answer. Yet, I think it is important that we really understand the depth of the answer. Why do we or why should we love God? Well, there are more answers to this question than could be answered in a lifetime. But, I will give the best answer I can...

He is incomparable. There is none like Him - II Samuel 7:22 says: *Therefore You are great, O Lord God; for none is like You, nor is there any God besides You...* No other religion has a God like ours. HE IS!

His ways are perfect. He is perfect - Psalm 18:30 says: *As for God, His way is perfect!*

He is our Rock and Shield - Psalm 18:30-31 says: *...He is a shield to all those who take refuge and put their trust in Him. For who is God except the Lord? Or who is the Rock save our God?* It says it right there...if we will take refuge... He will shield us. How many of us actually take refuge in Him?

He is the Creator of all things - This is covered in Genesis 1, Isaiah 40:12, 22 & 26 as well as countless other verses. What other God created the Universe?

He is Everlasting - Habakkuk 3:6 says: *He stood and measured the earth; He looked and shook the nations, and the eternal mountains were scattered and the perpetual hills bowed low. His ways are everlasting and His goings are of old.*

He is Just, True, Mighty, and Sovereign - Revelation 15:3 says: *...Mighty and marvelous are Your works, O Lord God the Omnipotent! Just and true are Your ways, O Sovereign of the ages.* Sing that for a while and you'll feel His presence all around you.

He is my Strength and my Song - When I am weak I know I can count on Him to be my Strength. Exodus 15:2 says: *the Lord is my Strength and my Song...* Keep reading that chapter alone for many reasons to love Him.

He loved us first - I John 4:19 says: *We love Him, because He first loved us.*

He is Omnipotent (All-Powerful) - Jeremiah 32:17 says: *alas, Lord God! Behold, You have made the heavens and the earth by your great power and by Your outstretched arm! There is nothing too hard for You.*

He is Omnipresent (Ever-Present) - Read Psalm 139:7-12. He is always here... He is always there. You are never alone. What other "god" can say that?

He is Omniscient (All-Knowing) - I John 3:20 says: *...For He is above and greater than our consciences (our hearts), and He knows and understands everything, nothing is hidden from Him.*

These are not even the tip of the iceberg... There is not enough time or words to tell all the reasons to love our God. He is: The Great I Am, The King of Kings, The Lord of Lords, Yahweh-jireh (my Provider), Yahweh-nissi (He reigns in victory), Yahweh-shalom (my Peace), Yahweh-Shammah (the Lord is here), Yahweh-Mekaddishkem (our Sanctifier), God Almighty, Heavenly Father, Abba (Daddy), Holy, Savior, Prince of Peace, Loving, Kind, Gentle, Patient, Worthy, Good, Gracious...

Do you see what I mean? I really could go on forever.

Called to Love

"You have heard that it was said, 'Love your neighbor and hate your enemy.' But I tell you: Love your enemies and pray for those who persecute you, that you may be sons of your Father in heaven. He causes His sun to rise on the evil and the good, and sends rain on the righteous and the unrighteous. If you love those who love you, what reward will you get? Are not even the tax collectors doing that? - Matthew 5:43-46

Who is our enemy?

I think this goes way deeper than the obvious. I would like to challenge you in your thinking and venture to say that it is not just those who have wounded us deeply. It can be someone who is a close friend or even a spouse.

Sure, they do not appear to be our enemy. However, if you look at the meaning of enemy, it means: *antagonistic, hostile, and belligerent.* A lot of marriages and close friendships can experience these emotions at one point or another.

It can be very hard to love someone who treats you badly or says hurtful things to you. Especially if that person is someone close to you, or that you respect. You expect more…

Unfortunately, we are in a sinful world and we all have baggage. We take the junk of our pasts with us wherever we go.

It's not always easy to **love our** enemies--even those close to us. It can be downright difficult. I struggle with this on a daily basis.

I believe the main reason it is difficult to "love" others is because we allow our "feelings" to get in the way. Our "feelings" (aka our flesh) will always steer us in the wrong direction. We must <u>choose</u> to love. We must submit our feelings to the foot of the cross… and leave them there! We must <u>choose</u> to love our "enemies". We must <u>choose</u> to love those who wrong us.

Love is a <u>choice</u> that we must MAKE each day.

Our friends, spouses, and loved ones will never deserve our love or do enough to earn it. They will **always** let us down. We must put our hearts, hope and trust in the Lord. He is the <u>ONLY</u> One Who will <u>never</u> leave us, <u>never</u> forsake us, <u>never</u> hurt us, and **always** love us. We must let go of our unrealistic expectations of others, and love them the way they are.

After all…

We are <u>CALLED</u> to love… and God loves <u>US</u> the way we are!

Once we understand that "feelings" have nothing to do with love, we will be better equipped to walk in Love.

Will it be easy?

No way!

It wasn't easy dying on a cross either!

Final Thoughts on Love

As I mentioned earlier, we must pursue an active relationship with the Father in order to ever walk in love to the capacity that we are meant to!

Every day we should:

Pray – This is something you can do under your breath all day long. You don't need some dramatic place and planned out script every day. I think we should have structured prayers that include: praise, worship, thankfulness, prayer for others, and prayer for ourselves. However, there may be days you only have time for what I like to call, "the on the go prayers." God is not offended. God is happy that we want to share our day with Him. I include Him in my grocery shopping, shows I want to watch, cooking dinner, etc. The point is talk to Him! Every day!

Read the Word – Not every one has an hour or two a day to spend in the Word. We all have some time though. Even five minutes. It is the best five minutes you will ever spend. It is your life source. It is the ONLY way to really know Who God is and His wonderful character.

If you are just starting out, I would suggest reading Psalms and/or Proverbs. They are great books and are filled with Life. Try memorizing one verse a week. Once you master that, try two, and so on. It takes practice to study the Word. There may be days you feel like nothing was gained. But, I promise you did. You just don't know it… yet. Trust me. I've been there.

Praise and Thanksgiving – You can listen to some praise music while driving, cooking, working, cleaning, exercising, or even a physical activity (sports). Believe it or not, when we listen to positive or faith-based music, it does wonders for our entire being. It renews our mind with the things of God. It reminds us to be thankful. It makes us want to praise the Lord. Find some good Christian music in the style that you like and cut loose. Anything that the world has, God has better, and then some.

When we begin to do all these things on a regular basis, we will start seeing major changes in our minds, attitudes, talk, and lives.

Then, one day, when we are not even thinking about it, we will have this big piece of fruit sticking out of our chest: the fruit of Love. The fruit that helps all the other fruit grow.

The first and most important fruit is LOVE.

Love - Study Guide

Let's Pray:

Lord, I want to thank You for Your Word. Thank You for loving me even when I am unlovable. Thank You for all that You do and have done for me. I am nothing without You and I need You to even breath. I love You, Lord, and I long to develop all the fruits of the spirit and to walk in love. Help me to get to know You better and more fully. Show me Who You are. I want to have a closer walk with You. I want to know You more and more every day. Thank You. I praise Your Holy and Precious Name. You are Worthy of all my praise. In Jesus' Mighty Name, Amen.

Memorize:

Above all, clothe yourselves with love, which binds us all together in perfect harmony. - Colossians 3:14

Dig Deeper:

Always be humble and gentle. Be patient with each other, making allowance for each other's faults <u>because of your love</u>. - Ephesians 4:2

I would say that I fail miserably on a daily basis with this one. By all means, please stop reading if you have mastered Ephesians 4:2.

For those of you who struggle with being humble, gentle and patient, let's dig deeper…

To be **humble** is to be: *submissive, meek, unassuming, polite, not proud or arrogant and modest.*

To be **gentle** is to be: *clement, peaceful, soothing, tender, lenient, merciful, mild, temperate, tame, quiet, and courteous.*

To be **patient** is to be: *uncomplaining, long-suffering, forbearing, calm, unruffled, unexcited, composed and untiring.* Patience is also able to: *bear provocation, annoyance, misfortune, delay, hardship, pain, etc., with fortitude and calm and without complaint, anger, or the like.*

Nope, not me!

I get aggravated, loud, impatient, tired, and angry with people. I do not always make allowances for the faults of others and people can really tick me off! LOL! I find this Scripture very challenging. However, then I think about how God looks past my faults and loves me no matter what. How can I deny someone the same courtesy?

How can we possibly deal with the ridiculous people we encounter each day? Better yet, how do we deal with those who are closest to us? They seem to be the ones who really push our buttons! The answer is in the Scripture as well…

…Because of your love…

Yes, Christ's love and strength is IN us, and if we choose to love, we CAN. We may need to try a bit harder dealing with some; however, we really can be gentle, kind, patient and humble with all people. We just need to realize it cannot be done through our own strength. We need to rely on the Lord to give us the strength!

Keep on asking and it will be given you; keep on seeking and you will find; keep on knocking and the door will be opened to you. - Matthew 7:7

We need to ask, seek and knock for what we need. I know that I know that I KNOW that my Daddy God is ALWAYS available and willing to assist me when I need it. It is the same for you. When we encounter difficult people or have to deal with someone on a regular basis that really annoys us, we need to refer to God's Word. We need to seek HIS help. We need to find our strength IN HIM.

And, NEVER give up!

And as for you, brethren, do not become weary or lose heart in doing right, but continue in well-doing without weakening. - 2 Thessalonians 3:13

This is the key... we cannot allow ourselves to grow weary in well doing. We cannot lose heart. God wants to develop patience, gentleness and humility in all of us; because He loves us and knows it is the only way to true peace, joy and happiness. How can we find peace, joy and happiness if we are living without patience and in offense, anger, annoyances and pride?

We cannot.

Only love can help us reach our goal.

Only our love for God and willingness to obey Him will even get us on the road. Once there, the only way to walk the road of peace, joy and happiness is through forgiveness, humility, gentleness, patience, and Christ's love in us pouring out TO others... especially difficult "others".

Scripture Study:

Look up the following Scriptures. I encourage you to really dig deep here and study them, look up any references and pray over them!

- John 13:34-35
- 1 John 4:7-8
- 1 Peter 4:8
- Mark 12:31
- Proverbs 10:12
- 1 Corinthians 13:1-13
- 1 John 4:18-21

- Romans 13:10
- Leviticus 19:18
- 1 Corinthians 16:14
- John 14:15
- Romans 12:9

And let's remember God's great love for us...

- John 3:16
- Psalm 36:5
- Luke 12:7
- Romans 8:37-39
- Jeremiah 29:11
- Romans 5:8
- Revelation 3:19
- Psalm 103 (whole chapter)

Also, for an even deeper study, look up the following words in your concordance: *love, God's love, loving others,* and study the Scripture references.

OK, So, Now What??

Sure, we have dug deep and thoroughly discussed all 9 fruits of the spirit, so now what?? Well, there is a choice that we must make each and every day of our lives: The choice to submit our will to God, or the choice to do it our way.

For all who are led by the Spirit of God are children of God. - Romans 8:14

Being led by the Holy Spirit means we are allowing Him to work in us, and giving God complete control over our lives. It is allowing God to be what He is--King. In a kingdom, the people obey the King-- period.

Unfortunately, in today's ever increasingly sin-filled culture submitting to anyone other than self is for mindless morons. I am here to say it is just the opposite. Submitting to God does not make you a mindless moron. Quite the contrary actually: It makes you wise, filled with peace, and keeps you on a path that leads to life.

God is All Powerful. He does not need us. He could have made us mindless beings that did His bidding. However, He created us with free will and all He desires is for us to come willingly to Him. He desires to break bread with us and have friendship.

Submitting to the Holy Spirit is an act of love in worship to our Daddy God. He wants us submitted BECAUSE He loves us. It is for our protection and welfare. He knows what is best for us more than we do and He does not have any pesky flesh in the way to blind us. All He has is pure love and great plans for us.

We must learn to submit to the Holy Spirit.

The Holy Spirit has several roles that He plays in our lives. Some of them require action by us and others are done regardless of our actions. It is important that we know them, so that we can better understand the Spirit and His ways.

The Holy Spirit's Roles...

Convict - the Holy Spirit convicts us of our sin. *(ref. John 16:7-11)*

Baptize - we are not only to be baptized with water, but with fire. The baptism of the Holy Spirit is a very powerful thing and no Believer should lack in this area. In many ways, failure to receive this power is what causes much grief in a Believer's life. ONLY the Holy Spirit leads us to a renewal and a deeper level with the Lord and an understanding that can give us. *(ref. 1Corinthians 12:13, 30)*

Rebirth - we are "born again" through the power of the Holy Spirit. We are new creatures in Christ. The old has passed away and the new has come. We no longer have to be ruled by sin. We now have the power to overcome sin through the power of the Holy Spirit. *(ref. John 3:1-8)*

Fill - another job of the Holy Spirit is to FILL us with His presence. However, the only way this can happen is IF we allow Him to, and yield to the will of the Father. Allowing the Spirit to control us is allowing God's WILL to be our will. It means letting go of ourselves and letting God mold us into His image. This is something that is all based on our own will. The Holy Spirit cannot lead us UNLESS we allow Him to! *(ref. Ephesians 5:18)*

Restrain - the Holy Spirit's presence in this world restrains evil. We think it's bad now... we have no clue! It would be a world filled with ONLY hate, lust, sin and an overwhelming wickedness the likes of which we have never seen. There would be NO good thing. There would be every evil thing you can imagine. There would be no hope. No mercy. Only Pain. Without the presence of the Holy Spirit this world would be run by evil and NO good thing would be here--period. *(ref. 2Thessalonians 2:6-12)*

Indwell - He is IN us. The Holy Spirit indwells in us when we receive Him. He makes the Word fully known to us. Even David knew Him and did not want to be separated from Him! *(ref. Colossians 1:25-27, Psalm 51:10-12)*

Seal - we are marked for lack of a better word… sealed as owned by the Living God. We are joint heirs with Jesus Christ. This is a HUGE thing. We are God's. NOTHING else can have us. ONLY the Holy Spirit can dwell IN us. No demon can harm us or possess us. *(ref. Ephesians 4:30)*

God wants us to understand the Holy Spirit's role in our lives. He wants us to yield to the power of the Holy Spirit and allow Him to lead us to a victorious and peace-filled life. He wants us to be FILLED with His presence.

So how does developing fruit tie into all of this?

Well, walking in the spirit is the ONLY way to produce fruit! We will ONLY produce healthy fruit in our lives as we submit our lives to the Lord and allow Him to lead us…

Who is Your Vine Dresser??

May Christ through your faith actually dwell in your hearts! May you be rooted deep in love and founded securely on love, That you may have the power and be strong to apprehend and grasp with all the saints what is the breadth and length and height and depth of it; That you may really come to know practically, through experience for yourselves, the love of Christ, which far surpasses mere knowledge; that you may be filled with all the fullness of God, and become a body wholly filled and flooded with God Himself! Now to Him Who, is able to do exceedingly abundantly above all that we dare ask or think [infinitely beyond our highest prayers, desires, thoughts, hopes, or dreams]–To Him be glory in the church and in Christ Jesus throughout all generations forever and ever. Amen (so be it). - Ephesians 3:17-21

Our roots SHOULD be grounded in LOVE. However, many times, we do not choose to ground ourselves in love and instead, we choose the ways, desires, and things of this world. When we allow our hearts to be moved away from the Will, Love and purposes of God, we are stepping away from the security of the Vine. This world can bring us down, cause us to lose our way, and bring anger, covetousness and the like to the doorway of our hearts.

We must CHOOSE to be rooted in love. We must CHOOSE to remain IN the Vine!

"I am the true vine, and My Father is the vine-dresser. Every branch in Me that does not bear fruit He takes away; and every branch that bears fruit He prunes, that it may bear more fruit. You are already clean because of the word which I have spoken to you. Abide in Me, and I in you. As the branch cannot bear fruit of itself, unless it abides in the vine, neither can you, unless you abide in Me. "I am the vine, you are the branches. He who abides in Me, and I in him, bears much fruit; for without Me you can do nothing. If anyone does not abide in Me, he is cast out as a branch and is withered; and they gather them and throw them into the fire, and

they are burned. If you abide in Me, and My words abide in you, you will ask what you desire, and it shall be done for you. By this My Father is glorified, that you bear much fruit; so you will be My disciples. - John 15:1-8

You see, when we submit to the Will, Word and Authority of God, we are allowing HIM to be our vine-dresser. On the contrary, when we take the steering wheel away from the Lord and take over, we become the vine-dressers. Once we take on the role that God should have, we kill fruit, ruin our trees and become useless, fruitless, unhappy, unsatisfied, and rebellious. There is NO joy in our own abilities. There is NO victory in our own abilities. ONLY through the strength, power, grace, and love of Christ can we find peace, joy, victory and abundant life. Outside of the TRUE VINE is nothing but pain, sadness, anger, sin, and danger.

How do we remain in the safety of the Vine?

"As the Father loved Me, I also have loved you; abide in My love. If you keep My commandments, you will abide in My love, just as I have kept My Father's commandments and abide in His love. "These things I have spoken to you, that My joy may remain in you, and that your joy may be full. This is My commandment, that you love one another as I have loved you. Greater love has no one than this, than to lay down one's life for his friends. You are My friends if you do whatever I command you. No longer do I call you servants, for a servant does not know what his master is doing; but I have called you friends, for all things that I heard from My Father I have made known to you. You did not choose Me, but I chose you and appointed you that you should go and bear fruit, and that your fruit should remain, that whatever you ask the Father in My name He may give you. These things I command you, that you love one another. - John 15:9-17

We must receive God's love, and abide in it.

We must obey His Word.

We must love others.

We were CREATED for God and to PRODUCE fruit. If we do not produce fruit, we are not living productive and obedient lives. Our purpose goes far beyond carpooling, eating, soccer practice, exercise, hobbies, work, activities, and the mundane tasks of every day life. We are a part of an army. We are soldiers for the Kingdom. Our lives need to reflect His purpose... His will... His love and we <u>must produce healthy fruit</u>! There are no more excuses. Seriously, we need to wake up and CHOOSE to walk in the spirit and let go of the things of this world. We need to be living testimonies before our children, friends, spouses, co-workers, relatives, and the world. They need to SEE us walking it out, making hard choices, denying our flesh and <u>ABIDING</u> in the safety of the Vine!

I ask again...

Who is <u>YOUR</u> Vine Dresser??

Pruning

"Beware of false prophets who come disguised as harmless sheep but are really vicious wolves. You can identify them <u>by their fruit,</u> that is, by the way they act. Can you pick grapes from thornbushes, or figs from thistles? <u>A good tree produces good fruit,</u> and a bad tree produces bad fruit. <u>A good tree can't produce bad fruit, and a bad tree can't produce good fruit.</u> So every tree that does not produce good fruit is chopped down and thrown into the fire. Yes, just as you can identify a tree by its fruit, so you can identify people by their actions. - Matthew 7:15-20

By now, you are aware that the Fruit of the Spirit is the character and proof of our walks with the Lord. As we grow, we bear good fruit. On the flip side, when we are in error, or falling away, we do not produce good fruit. Our trees are healthy and growing, or barren and rotten.

My desire is to have a healthy AND growing tree at all times, and to help others have the same.

There is significance in the way God's Word uses the references "Fruit of the Spirit" and other phrases like: good fruit, trees, pruning, branches, etc.

Pruning means, *to cut off or cut back parts of for better shape or more fruitful growth.*

I want to dig deeper into the pruning aspect of growing a healthy fruit tree.

Those who grow trees understand the pruning process. However, those of us who only go to the store and buy the fruit that growers have poured their blood, sweat, and tears into growing, do not understand the value of the pruning process.

You see, without proper training and pruning, fruit trees will not grow into their full potential. They will lack. However, when they are pruned and trained, they will not only yield higher quality fruit, but for a longer lifespan.

Interesting Facts about Fruit Trees and the Training/Pruning Process:

Pruning helps the <u>entire tree</u> to be stronger, healthier, and more productive.

Pruning also helps <u>remove</u> dead branches, disease, and broken limbs.

Training fruit trees while young will <u>help</u> them to avoid problems later in life.

Fruit trees that are not properly trained and pruned are more likely to succumb to disease and breakage from fruit loads and storms.

Even with pruning there is purpose. Each cut has significance. Each cut helps grow and shape each tree differently.

This is amazing to me. Even us, God's Beloved, are each different, and will require different pruning processes. Our trees are all for different purposes, thus, our trees will require different forms of maintenance.

Some of us may flourish more in one fruit area than another. However, we are all ONE Body and we each have value.

Keep in mind though; <u>our fruit will all have similarities</u>. Just as an apple is an apple. Love is love. And, when the Scripture says, *"You will know them by their fruit..."* Well, that is where we all exhibit the same character traits that our Lord has placed within the foundation of each fruit.

Yes, pruning involves cutting, and removing--and can be painful. However, it is one of the most important aspects of growing a strong, healthy, fruit-bearing tree that will not only bring glory to God, but victory to our lives!

Narrow is the Path

Enter through the narrow gate; for wide is the gate and spacious and broad is the way that leads away to destruction, and many are those who are entering through it.

But the gate is narrow (contracted by pressure) and the way is straitened and compressed that leads away to life, and few are those who find it.- Matthew 7:13-14

This is a very interesting statement that Jesus made. The word **gate** comes from the Greek word **pules** and means; *a door, gate, large door or entrance of a large city. To be distinguished from, a common door.*

This tells me that there are two places these gates take us…Heaven and hell.

The scary part of this is the "few" part. There are MANY people who "claim" to be Christians, yet their lives do not show it. We should be certain that we are on the right path. Our flesh will always try to lead us back to the easier (broad) path. Our Daddy in Heaven did not leave us to figure this out on our own. Jesus clearly tells us in these Scriptures, how to know if someone is walking down the right path.

Knowing that it is by their fruit that we will be able to discern makes it much easier to know WHO we should be listening to and allowing to speak into our lives.

Questions to Consider:

It is VITAL to your spiritual health to pay close attention to WHOM you let speak into your life. You cannot just listen to every person that claims to be a Christian…or who feeds your fleshly tendencies.

Do they walk in the Spirit or Flesh? A person who is walking in the spirit will be growing. A person who is walking in the spirit will be very uncomfortable listening to music or watching things that glorify sin and the flesh.

They will be convicted when they say or do something that was an act of their flesh. God corrects those that are His…just like a good parent should.

Does their talk line up with the Word? This requires YOU to read the Word. You can not take another persons' word for it… no matter WHAT position they hold.

Anyone can quote Scriptures and throw out a believable interpretation. The devil himself used God's own Word against Jesus when he tried to tempt him!

We need to be VERY careful…VERY alert…and Pray about everything!

Do they walk the walk? They should be living the Christian life in public AND in private. This will be hard to know unless you are close to this person.

Another thing you should ALWAYS do is PRAY! Ask Daddy. Wait. He WILL reveal His Truth to you. It may not always be easy to hear…and you may have to walk away from a friendship or place, but you will be OK. God will help you through it and you will grow from the experience.

Consider this

It is NOT easy to walk the narrow road. It can be lonely and scary. However, no matter how hard it is, we know that pearly gates, streets of gold, and a loving God lay at the end of the narrow road.

We know that when we fail, we can get up, dust off, and get right back on that road with the help of our Daddy God. We must be WILLING and ALWAYS alert!

Be self-controlled and alert. Your enemy the devil prowls around like a roaring lion looking for someone to devour. - 1Peter 5:8

Am I saying we should not love those that are in error? Absolutely NOT! However, we can NOT allow them to influence US. We need to be a light to THEM…and you should pray for them. You should NOT become involved with them to the point where they begin to cause you confusion or to slip.

The Broad Road

This road leads to sin, sadness, separation from God, and ultimately hell: A horrible and extremely wicked and unhappy place. Unfortunately, when we are on the broad path we don't see it that way. It's easy and fun. It's all about the flesh and self.

Even Christians can be lead astray onto the broad path. If you see yourself making compromises, sinning in a particular area frequently, and adapting yourself to this world and its ways, you may want to step back, do a spiritual inventory, confess to the Lord, turn from the sin, and find your way back to the narrow path. On it you will make harder choices, but your ending will be MUCH better!

How do we get ourselves on the narrow path?

If you are saved, it's about choices. Who do you serve? Who do you want to represent? Who do you really love? Once you decide that Jesus is the ONLY path you want to take, turn from your sin *(ref. 2 Chronicles 7:14)*, repent *(ref. 1 John 1:9)*, and get back on track.

Life on the narrow path takes guts and courage. You may not "think" you have what it takes, but you do. I know you do. I know, because, God doesn't make junk and He doesn't make mistakes!

Make sure that your life is being lived for the One Who gave His Life for you! Walk the narrow road and STAY on it!

It's All About Choices...

In closing, I just want to remind you that God loves you and only wants the best for you. He created you to love you. He wants your life to be a living testimony of His grace, love, and mercy. He wants you to walk in VICTORY.

True growth can only develop when we choose to allow God to work in our hearts and help us become the flourishing fruit bearing trees He created us to be.

Habits that Promote Spiritual Growth

Develop an Active Prayer Life. This requires taking the time to talk to God every day. I do not mean with a list of wants either. We need to spend time with Him and include Him in our daily life.

Praise Him. This is a very important aspect of spiritual growth. We must cultivate a heart of thanksgiving. Praise and worship are also great tools in helping us to overcome trials, doubt, and heartache. We enter into His gates with thanksgiving and into His courts with praise. *(ref. Psalm 100)* Thanksgiving and praise are where He abides! *(ref. Psalm 22:3)*

Read and Memorize the Word. To really know God and have a relationship with Him requires reading and studying His Word. Everything we need to know about Him, life, spiritual growth, and how to live here are in His Word. Read it. Study it. Memorize it. Make it a priority.

Obey. The Holy Spirit will not yell at us. It is a still small voice. This world is very loud. It is a LOT easier to "hear" the world, flesh, and sin. However, we all CAN hear the conviction of the Holy Spirit. We are His sheep and we hear His voice. When you get convicted, obey, repent, and turn from whatever it is. If we continue in our sin, it will be harder to turn later. Plus, eventually, the Lord will stop telling us... He will just let us do what we want.

It's all about choices...

Let me leave you with this:

If you really love Me, you will obey My commands. - John 14:15

Final Study Guide

Let's Pray:

Lord, thank You for Your Word. I am amazed again at the life it brings! Thank You that You have called me to greater things than the mundane things of life. Thank You that You have provided me with strength and the ability to remain in Your Vine. Lord, I turn over my shears to You! I want You to be my vine-dresser! Prune me, Lord, and develop me into the flourishing, fruit-bearing tree that You created me to be. I want You to guide me down the paths You chose for me in this life. Help me to see Your way clearly and never leave the safety of the narrow path! I love You, Lord! Thank you for loving me! In Jesus' Mighty Name, Amen.

Memorize:

It is God who enables us, along with you, to stand firm for Christ. He has commissioned us, and he has identified us as his own by placing the Holy Spirit in our hearts as the first installment that guarantees everything he has promised us. – 2 Corinthians 1:21-22

Dig Deeper:

I am sure by now that I have made it clear that the only way to have a fruit-filled life is to walk in the spirit. We must choose to live obedient lives and trust that the God we love and serve knows better than us. We must stop being bottle fed and become the mature men and women of God that we were created to be.

We must make the choice to live completely and unabashedly for the One Who chose to be undeservedly beaten, spit on, and ultimately put to death for us.

Is it a life of no sorrow?

No. There is sin in this world and with it pain and sorrow. There is no escape from that until we get to Heaven.

Is there peace?

You bet there is. When you are a TRUE follower of the Living God, you have a peace and assurance that nothing this world has can offer... not money, not power, not anything.

Is it easy?

Heck no--Especially in this culture. Everything around us is screaming against walking with the Lord God All Mighty. I will warn you, walking the walk is NOT for the faint of heart!

Is it worth it?

YES! Think about what Jesus did for YOU and me! He walked more than a mile in our shoes. He faced pain and ridicule for us. He loved us enough to do what it took to allow us the opportunity to live eternity in Heaven... *if we choose to.*

I want nothing... *nothing* more than to live a life that pleases my Daddy God. At the end of my days, I want to her Him say, *"Well done!"* NOTHING in this world matters more than that!

But I say, walk and live [habitually] in the Spirit [responsive to and controlled and guided by the Spirit]; then you will certainly not gratify the cravings and desires of the flesh. - Galatians 5:16

Scripture Study:

Look up the following Scriptures. I encourage you to really dig deep here and study them, look up any references and pray over them!

- 2 John 1:4-9
- 1 Peter 1:14-16
- 1Corinthians 6:19-20
- 1 John 3:24
- John 15 (whole chapter)
- 1 Corinthians 6:19
- Proverbs 16:7
- John 14:6
- Colossians 2:10
- Ephesians 2:10
- John 14:16
- Galatians 5 (whole chapter)
- 2 Corinthians 5:17
- Psalm 119 (whole chapter)
- Matthew 6:24
- Joshua 24:14
- Proverbs 10:8
- Ephesians 5:8
- Psalm 51:10-12
- John 16:7-11
- John 3:1-8
- Romans 8:38-39

- 1Corinthians 12:13
- Colossians 1:25-27
- 2Thessalonians 2:6-12
- Titus 3:5

Also, for an even deeper study, look up the following words in your concordance: *obey, obedience, walking in the spirit, submit, submitted,* and study the Scripture references.

About the Author

Lara is a wife, mom, homeschooler, published author, ministry leader, speaker, and supreme multi-tasker! She is honest and forthright in her writing, and shares her heart, struggles, joys, pains, and the many lessons she has learned on her journey–in a relatable way that pulls no punches.

Besides all that, she is a chauffeur, friend, maid, chef, business owner, lover, confidant, mentor, teacher, seeker, nurse, boo-boo kisser, cat lover, coffee drinker, Starbucks follower, Mexican food addict, jean loving, sometimes loud mouth, opinionated, outspoken, web designer, iphone carrier, a teensy bit anal retentive, chocoholic, Survivor fan, Bible believing, animal lover, reptile and crawly things hating, speed walking, honest, working her way back to skinny jeans, and... One heck of a strong woman! (Among other things)

"O God, listen to my cry! Hear my prayer! From the ends of the earth, I cry to You for help when my heart is overwhelmed. Lead me to the towering rock of safety, for You are my safe refuge, a fortress where my enemies cannot reach me. Let me live forever in Your sanctuary, safe beneath the shelter of Your wings!" – Psalm 61:1-4

You can find her…

Her Blog:
LaraVelez.com

On Smashwords (Digital and Print Versions of her Books):
smashwords.com/profile/view/Lvelez

Amazon (Kindle and Print Books):
amazon.com/author/laravelez

On Facebook:
facebook.com/LaraVelez.Author

On Twitter:
@Faithful_Mommie

On Pinterest:
pinterest.com/faithful_mommie

You can also find her work on…

Moms of Faith:
momsoffaith.com

Real Christian Wives:
realchristianwives.com

Proverbs 31 Wife Handbook:
proverbs31wifehandbook.com

Made in the USA
Middletown, DE
01 May 2018